D0998488

UNDER YOUR FEET

Mound Builder depicted with copper jewels and an axe as excavated in Western Kentucky in 1938. This interpretation made by the writer, Blanche Busey King, and her husband, Colonel Fain White King, research Director of Archæology of Kentucky. The entire mound containing this copper was excavated by them and their staff of archæologists

UNDER YOUR FEET

The Story of the American Mound Builders

By

BLANCHE BUSEY KING

Illustrated

BOOKS FOR LIBRARIES PRESS
FREEPORT, NEW YORK

First Published 1939
Reprinted 1971

INTERNATIONAL STANDARD BOOK NUMBER:
0-8369-5742-3

LIBRARY OF CONGRESS CATALOG CARD NUMBER:
73-152990

PRINTED IN THE UNITED STATES OF AMERICA

E
73.
K56

To my Father and Mother—
——My best friends

PREFACE

PEOPLE are becoming more archæologically conscious every day. In my contact with the public at one site which is now in its seventh year, with thirty to forty thousand visitors annually and the number increasing all the time, I have been asked thousands of questions. The purpose of this book is to answer some of these many questions, adhering to the most recent scientific data.

Primarily, it is an earnest effort to tell in simple language the story of the Mound Building Peoples of the Mississippi Valley, with comparisons of my work in other countries.

This book is presented with grateful acknowledgment to my husband, Colonel Fain White King, and to Dr. Fay Cooper Cole, Chairman of the Department of Anthropology, University of Chicago, and his wife, Mabel Cook Cole, who crystallized by discussion my writing of it.

Over a period of years, in my problems of research, I have turned to Dr. Nels Christian Nelson, Curator of Prehistoric Archæology at the American Museum of Natural History, New York City, and notwithstanding he is one of the busiest of men, he has always given invaluable assistance, as has my good friend, Dr. Alês Hrdlička, Curator of Anthropology at the Smithsonian Institution, Washington, D.C. To Dr. George Gustav Heye, Chairman and Director of the Museum of the American Indian of the Heye Foundation, New York City, I also owe many thanks for his kindness in offering suggestions and photographic material and in co-operating to the fullest extent. And to the following for their many courtesies: President Clement Clarence Williams, Lehigh University, Bethlehem, Pennsylvania; Dr. George Frederick Arps, Dean of the Graduate School, Columbus, Ohio; Dr. John Reed Swanton, Ethnologist, Bureau of Ethnology, Washington, D.C.; Dr. Diamond Jenness, Chief of the Division of Anthropology, National Museum of Canada; Dr. Donald Scott, Director of Peabody Museum of Archæology and Ethnology, Harvard University; Dr. Clark Wissler, Curator of Anthropology, Natural History Museum, New York City; Dr. Henry Clyde Shetrone, Director of Columbus Museum, Columbus, Ohio; Dr. Charles E. Brown, Director of the State Historical Museum, Madison, Wisconsin; Dr. Phineas Lawrence Windsor, Director of the Library, University of Illinois, Urbana, Illinois; Dr. Van Andrews, Cairo, Illinois., Miss Effie Lansden, Cairo, Illinois and Mr. G. M. Pedley, Director Division of Publicity, Frankfort, Kentucky.

BLANCHE BUSEY KING

Wickliffe, Kentucky
June 1939

CONTENTS

ILLUSTRATIONS

[xi]

ILLUSTRATIONS

[xii]

UNDER YOUR FEET

CHAPTER I

UNDER YOUR FEET

HAVE you ever had the wanderlust to see some of the strange places in the world—the great monuments like Stonehenge, Carnac, Easter Island, the Pyramids, Ur, Timgad? Or are you equally fascinated with the beckoning of a little path through the woods, and a winding road? Were you ever in the mood of this charming song by Le Gallienne?

> "I meant to do my work today—
> But a little bird sang in the apple tree,
> And a butterfly flitted across the field,
> And all the leaves were calling me;
> And the wind went sighing over the land,
> Tossing the grasses to and fro,
> And a rainbow held out its shining hand—
> So what could I do—
> So what could I do—
> But laugh—laugh and go."

Do you ever speculate about places while traveling, such as the great castles on the Rhine, or the huge monasteries on bleak hilltops in Italy? In your American travels, have you ever noticed mounds of various heights, scattered here and there, and said to yourself, "I wonder who made that and what it contains? I certainly should like to dig in there and see." Andrew Marvel once wrote:

> "The grave's a fine and private place
> But none, I think, do there embrace."

Well, the Mound Builder did embrace, once upon a time, and thrilled at sunsets, was gay and sad, even as you and I.

Wherever the Mississippi and Ohio rivers and their great tributaries stretch, there are mounds, great earthworks, monuments of a long and forgotten past that we are just remembering. Each year that we excavate we learn more about these prehistoric peoples.

Monuments are fast crumbling away; folklore and tradition, however, still remain. It is amazing how the mounds of the Mound Builder are still intact in many places, while numerous monuments of marble and stone have fallen into the dust.

To understand the monuments of the Mound Builder, we should know something about the great megalithic monuments in France and Great Britain.

Although I have traveled all over Brittany, I have always come back to a beautiful little spot where the River Laïta meets the sea. It is eight miles from a railroad in Finistère. The property at this little place has been in a Monsieur Portier's family for over two hundred years. Notwithstanding the Breton people are very reticent and slow to make friends, they were most kind to me in every way. They still cling to the customs and beliefs of their forefathers in mystery and magic.

I used to like to sit on some old steps, hewn out of the rock, and watch the tide creep up to my feet, and in the distance see the fishermen in their boats shoot the rapids around the great cliffs, where the river joined the sea, on their way to fish for lobster in the ocean.

As I moved higher up the steps, away from the seemingly imperceptible rising of the tide, I thought of Victor Hugo's hero in *Toilers of the Sea,* and what courage he must have had to permit the tide to cover him. America seemed far away; at my back, I heard "Time's winged chariot hurrying near."

When I first stayed in Brittany, there were no electric lights; but shortly before I left the next year, electricity was installed and we had a celebration in honor of the great event. Day and night the new lights blazed, inside and outside, in outbuildings, and on gate-posts! Knowing the habitual frugality of the French people, I was amazed at this apparent waste and extravagance. I suggested to Madame Portier that the bills might be expensive, but she replied proudly, *"Mais non, Madame! Cela ne fait rien. La Municipalité l'addition payera."* She seemed so happy about it that I didn't feel it was my place to disillusion her. Two years later, when I returned, promptly at nine-thirty (twilight is slow descending in Brittany) all lights went out. I thought I was back in the days of summer resorts in Michigan where all lights were put out at ten o'clock;

and if one didn't have a flashlight one was in danger of breaking a leg getting home—if he weren't already there.

The next day I asked what happened to the lights. *"Hélas!"* Madame explained to me, *"l'électricité est très, très cher!"*

I used to love to watch Madame's coiffe de Lorient flying in the breeze, and her feet go in and out like little mice beneath her full black skirt, as she directed the gardener trimming the rose trees. Then hastily going to the lobster pot down at the river, she would draw out a lobster for *"Homard du Kari,"* the most delicious of lobster dishes and *le spécialité du Hôtel.*

The Breton people love celebrations—market days, pardons, weddings, dancing; and it is a beautiful sight to see them in their holiday attire. At the ball to celebrate the electric lights, I danced with some of my *bonnes,* and although I pride myself on being a pretty good dancer, their custom of moving rapidly in a circle, without reversing through an entire dance, made me glad to sit down when it was over. However, *le cidre* and music are an exciting combination, and I was up and away whirling with the rest when the next dance started. We danced until the wee small hours of the morning, and the favorite music, in deference to me, was the only American piece they knew, called "Hallelujah." It was fortunate that I liked it years before when it was published; otherwise a whole evening dancing to the tune of "Hallelujah" would have been a little too much. But to return to prehistoric matters again.

It is thought that the great monuments of Carnac and Stonehenge were erected about 3000 B. C. These represent herculean toil. Large numbers of men, tools of stone, huge tree trunks, and tough rope made of plaited hide must have transported and erected the great stones in place. Some of the stone axes and deer antler tools left by the ancient builders resemble those used by the Mound Builder in the Mississippi Valley.

In the Breton tongue, these monuments are called dolmens, meaning stone table, and menhirs, which translated is end stone. Dolmens are large stones which were built into rooms and galleries that were used for funeral chambers, while menhirs are tall stones, similar to our monuments. These were placed in rows or alignments which terminated in a circle or cromlech. There is a north-easterly orientation in the parallel rows or alignments of these menhirs, which follows the course of the sun. In burials of the Mound Builder, a similar orientation is found. The deduction is, therefore, that both peoples were sun worshipers.

One may see dolmens and menhirs in various parts of France, but the finest of these great megalithic monuments are to be found in Brittany. Megalithic builders were active during the last part of the Neolithic period. On various routes to Carnac, on the shores of Quiberon Bay, stretching as far as the eye can see, are thousands of menhirs and dolmens.

[5]

Near Ménec stands the great Dolmen of Saint
Michel. This tumulus consists of a number of tombs or
chambers. The huge, central funeral chamber was made
of enormous granite blocks. In it a beautiful necklace,
similar to our turquoise, was found, and, in addition,
thirty-nine beautifully polished ceremonial axes, seven
of which had been purposely broken, no doubt to permit the spirit to escape. Similarly, in the mound burials, we find in some of the "killed" pottery a small
hole punched to release the spirit. The superstition is
that they were to accompany the owner to the new land,
as their work on earth was at an end, and the great
spirit would restore them to perfection on the arrival
of the deceased at the end of his journey. Indications
show that animals were slain to accompany their mas-
ters into the next world, as animal bones were found
in direct association with human bones in the tombs.
Flint, tools, and potsherds similar to our American
prehistoric excavations were also found. In the Musée
de Kernuz, the Musée de Vannes, and various other
museums in Brittany one may see fine specimens of
this Neolithic art.

Near Locmariaquer is one of the largest menhirs
known. It lies prone, broken into four great pieces. It
is said to have weighed over 342 tons, stood 67 feet
high in the original, and was one of the most beautiful
of megalithic monuments. Tables des Marchands is a
magnificent dolmen, and is supported on one end by a
cone-shaped menhir, on the inside of which are strange

engravings, which, according to some scientists, represent fields of wheat, heavy with grain, with the figure of the sun in the center. At Le Rocher, the signs on the megalithic monuments have caused much discussion. The serpent and the ax seem to predominate as ornaments in the majority of these monuments.

Near Pont-l'Abbé there are numerous small menhirs, and these are thought to represent male and female idols. On Easter Island a number of interesting menhirs or gods may be seen representing the human form and face. One wonders if they were images of the dead, just as we conjecture about face bowls that we excavate in the Mississippi Valley.

In Stonehenge and Avebury, one may see England's great prehistoric stone monuments. At Stonehenge, the early Breton circle with the avenue is easily recognizable. Although having common origin, no doubt, with Carnac, Stonehenge has many distinguishing features that set it in a class by itself. It is most impressive and the alignments are thought to be agricultural calendars and indicative of sun worship. The great stones are very imposing at sunrise and sunset, when the sun is low on the horizon and each stone is tipped with light.

In Wiltshire are the surviving menhirs of Avebury's great outer circle. Originally there were seven hundred huge stones, arranged in three circles; but the ruthless vandalism of centuries has resulted in their disappearance. It is interesting to see two large stones standing

[7]

like huge sentinels near a cottage. Many fine flints, pottery, gold and amber were found in the English excavations.

Near Bagneaux and Tregunc, in Brittany, are large dolmens, and at Kercado there is a huge underground dolmen, with a central hall, supported by menhirs, and a ceiling made from a single block of stone. They are also to be found at Lufang, Pierres Plates, Le Lizo, and Le Rocher—in fact, they are scattered everywhere in that region.

There are many legends and traditions concerning Carnac. Local superstition invests the whole region with curious tales, similar to the Celtic traditions of Ireland and Wales. Being particularly fond of folk tales, I enjoyed hearing these stories. One tale told to me by an old woman spinning in the sun was that they believed, unless special food was prepared and placed on the table of the dolmens, their crops would not be productive. According to legend, the menhirs were pagan soldiers whom Saint Cornély had turned into stone. Every Christmas at midnight they left their places to drink at the streams. Many of the country folk believed that anyone watching this miracle would meet with great misfortune. In spite of this tradition, I attempted to see the miracle, but was not successful.

According to the folk tales or tradition, Saint Cornély was traveling around the world in an ox-cart, carrying the blessings of God everywhere, when some heathen soldiers, wishing to kill him, pursued him. He arrived at Carnac and said: "It is here that I will stop; it is here that I will dwell." Then he hid in the ear of an ox and changed all the pursuing soldiers to stone. That is the reason one sees long aisles of stones, standing to the north of Carnac, and that often in the night specters or ghosts walk down the aisles, who were once soldiers of Cornély.

The Bretons also have a belief that Kerions, or very small strong dwarfs, lived in the dolmens. A common expression even now is "Strong as a Kerion." According to tradition, the Kerions still return to their old habitations in the dolmens, and woe to anyone who troubles them, for he will die swiftly and surely!

Oftentimes ghostly animals are to be met on bridges and it is believed one may only escape them by hastening to one of the near-by roadside shrines which are to be found all along the roads in Brittany.

In many sections, the natives speak an ancient Celtic tongue similar to Gaelic and Welsh. One time I looked at a little girl's book. It was printed both in French and Gaelic. Some of the people do not speak French, and like Ireland with England they oftentimes have their differences with France. During the Great War, however, they fought valiantly, shoulder to shoulder with the rest of France and today almost every town has its war memorial, some, as in Auray, being quite imposing. There may be only two hundred people in the village but twenty-five names on the shaft tell its silent story.

There are so many wonderful monuments in the world. To me the impressive arches of the great aqueducts in England and Italy are among the finest gifts that the Romans have left us. In Italy, on the Appian Way to Hadrian's Villa, and thence to Tivoli, one may see the great arches of Aqua Claudia in the distance, which carried water from springs in the neighborhood of Tivoli to Rome, centuries ago.

But to return to Brittany. When I said *"Au revoir"* to a very old Parisian lady who lived there, she shook her head sadly and said, *"Adieu."* Émile Pessard has composed a beautiful French song, *"L'Adieu du Matin."* I never sing it without thinking of this lovely old French lady who, because she was so very old, said *"Adieu"* instead of *"Au revoir."*

> "Time goes, you say? Ah, no!
> Alas, time stays; we go."

Great monuments in Europe, Egypt, and other countries are fascinating, but the romance and study of American mounds are equally inviting and should be more interesting to us, because they represent a chapter of our prehistory. The American Indian gave us much of the food we enjoy, and a number of our customs.

CHAPTER II

ORIGIN

INVARIABLY people ask, "Who was the Mound Builder?" "When did he come here?" "Where did he come from?" The consensus of opinion is that he, or rather the parent stem, came to America across the Bering Strait, between Northeastern Asia and Alaska.

"In Pliocene and Pleistocene times, Bering Strait was bridged by land several times. The way from the Old World to the New was open to Pleistocene man, if he cared to take it. He almost certainly did take it, and his fossil remains will yet be found in America." [1]

"The chief deduction of American anthropology, in the substance of which all serious students concur, is that this continent was peopled essentially from Northeastern Asia. The deduction is based on the facts that man could not have originated in the New World, and hence must have come from the Old; that the American aborigines are throughout of one fundamental race, the nearest relatives of which exist to this day over wide parts of northern and eastern Asia; and that the only practicable route for man in such a cultural stage as he must have been in at the time of his first coming to America was that *between Northeastern Asia and Alaska.*" [2]

The question of when he came to America is answered by Dr. N. C. Nelson: "However, taking into consideration all the facts set forth, the only conclusion that now seems warranted is that man did not reach the American continent until sometime after, but probably incidental to, the general disruption caused by the ice-retreat, and that he came as the bearer of the partially developed Neolithic culture, somewhere between 5,000 and 10,000 years ago. If, on palæontological grounds, more time than this must be granted, then—in keeping with the suggestion made in *Natural History* in 1919—the most that the archæologist can concede at present is that possibly we have in America very faint traces of the Solutrean culture stage, of which the Folsom, N.M., discovery may be an example. But even this admission still leaves the antiquity of man in America as *essentially post-glacial*." [3]

According to the French Jesuit Fathers, a Huron woman on the plains of Tartary was found who had been sold from tribe to tribe until she had passed from the Bering Strait into Central Asia.

Frank Boas writes: "The physical relationship of the American native to the east Asiatic is closer than that to any other race. Straight, dark hair; wide, rather flat face; heavy nose; and the tendency to a Mongoloid eye are common to both of them. Locally, types are found that are so much alike that it would be rather difficult to say whether an individual is an *Asiatic or an American*." [4]

The Aleutian Islanders navigate the intervening ocean between Asia and America. The Eskimo, the last comer in his two types, is a blood relation of the Indian and is a link between Asia and America, according to Dr. Alês Hrdlička.[5]

Most of us are a little vague on the subject of Alaska and the Aleutian Islands. Alaska is five times the size of Texas and one-fifth the size of the United States. There is a great variance in the temperature, some parts reaching 40 to 50 degrees below zero while in the Aleutian Islands it doesn't get as cold.

The Aleutian group is common stock to both Asia and America. Intermixture of vocabularies and dialects, due to migrations over a long period of time, proves intimate affinities between tribes on both sides of the Strait. The Eskimo appears to be a later offshoot from the same old stock that gave us the American Indian. "Probably our greatest hope in elucidating the early history of the Eskimo lies in archæology. Although their culture distinguishes them from all Indian tribes, yet this culture varies considerably in different regions." [6] There was no large migration like the exodus of the children of Israel,[7] but only small groups at a time, or relatively small dribblings over several millennia, either on foot or by boat.

Some of the prehistoric peoples used skin boats, similar to those of the Eskimos today. They made a frame of wicker over which they stretched caribou skins. Sometimes the skin was wrapped over the top, making it much easier to navigate in a rough sea than in an open boat. These were called kayaks. Sometimes sealskin was used as a sail. Boats were also formed out of the trunk of a tree, hollowed by fire with the help of primitive flint or shell axes. They were of various sizes, from a tiny bark capable of holding one person, similar to the ones used today by flower sellers at Xochimilico in Mexico, to large boats manned by thirty or forty paddlers. But long portages made by wooden canoes were impracticable, so they used canoes of birch which were light and graceful and could pass quickly along the great waterways.

In Glasgow, Scotland, a prehistoric canoe was discovered twenty-five feet below the surface of the Clyde River. It had been hewn out of a single oak. Near the prow was found a highly polished celt or stone ax.

The Mound Builder was an Indian—not the historic Indian, but a prehistoric Indian. He belonged to the Yellow-Brown Race.[8] He was a Mongoloid and from research we learn that he was of a tawny copper hue. Different tribes, however, were fairer than others. They were born white but due to exposure to the sun and rubbings of wolf oil and other fats which they believed made them strong, they became much darker. A Jesuit historian made this statement, but according to anthropological findings, no Mongoloid is completely white.

"The Indian type is distinguishable in one way or another from its nearest Mongoloid relations and at the same time is separable, according to some authorities, into about ten or more less distinct varieties, which, as in the case of languages, may or may not have developed since immigration took place." [9]

The American Indian, in all his varieties, is a descendant from a primitive Mongolian type of man, whose stem was evolved before the close of the Pleistocene period.[10]

Some think that the Mound Builder, the ancient Mexican, Aztec, and Toltec, and the Natchez historic Indian, came from the same stock. All groups on this hemisphere were of the same original stock; however, the Mound Builder belonged to a higher civilization than most of the historic Indians and was comparable to the Southwestern Pueblos in development of culture. According to Dr. Clark Wissler, the development of the American aborigines in the lower Mississippi Valley drainage basin, with its exotic ceramics, may yet be found to have culminated at the same time as the pueblo developments in New Mexico and Arizona, about 1200 A. D., and of Maya land about 1000 A. D.

The Mound Builder had many and varied headdresses but no hats as we designate them today. Time is not supposed to affect hair, but it is very subject to chemical reactions, such as the blonde and henna rinses of today. In burials, especially in caves, the atmospheric conditions, salts and chemical influences very often change the hair from a dark coloring to various shades of red. This has also been noted in burials in Peru and Egypt.

Schroeinfurth, in 1874, stated that the "Dunkes" imparted auroral tints to their hair by freely bedewing it with cow's urine, and subsequently washing it with a generous application of dung and ashes, in the form of a pomade. The ammoniacal and other alkaline constituents of the pomade and wash acted upon the oily pigments of the hair. Today we are still tinting hair. The beautician's art changes dark locks to light and vice versa.

Years ago, when I visited the catacombs in Rome, a facetious but delightful old monk acted as guide. He entertained us with stories about the various burials and told how people took bones and hair as souvenirs. Around one long-departed burial he wove quite a story. She had red hair, and he speculated at great length about the possibilities of her domestic life. But I couldn't seem to capture his illusions. Instead, these lines from *An Epitaph,* by Andrew Marvel, ran through my mind:

> "Modest as morn, as mid-day bright,
> Gentle as evening, cool as night:
> 'Tis true; but all too weakly said;
> 'Twas more significant, she's dead."

To what race did the Mound Builder belong? The indications are that Mound Builders were tribes of American Indians of the same race with the tribes now living; that they reached a stage of advancement about equal to that of the Pueblo Indians; that they were flourishing about a thousand years ago; and that at least in the tribes near the Gulf of Mexico were preserved some of their customs and some of their lineage till after the discovery of America by Columbus. These opinions are in accordance with a paper written for Congrès International des Americanists in 1877.

Columbus classified the Indian as obviously Asiatic, and although this opinion was later disputed by the mediæval scholars,[11] his views have now been proven correct.

The Indian had a well-developed form and straight features. "They were superior in height, well-made, well-proportioned, good-tempered, of sound constitution, quick, strong, active; in a word, in bodily qualities they are in no way our inferiors; they yielded nothing to us, in short, if indeed they do not have the advantage or surpass us." [12] We find from the skeletal material here, that they were not superior to us in height, a male five feet eleven being the tallest that we have excavated. On the whole, the skeletal material averages about one and one-half inches less than the average stature today.

Cranial deformations have been found in many countries, such as Scandinavia, Caledonia, Germany, and France. The cradle board was used by many prehistoric peoples. Flattening the head was a common practice with certain tribes of the Indian as well. To flatten the child's head, a piece of animal skin was filled with sand. It was then strapped to the cradle board. The cradle board was covered with many finely frayed fibers of cedar bark and fitted with a head board, projecting beyond the face and bound to the child's back to protect it from injury. This was covered with pliant deerskin, bound tightly by a leather band passing through holes in the cradle board and attached to the mother. Other pads were placed under the head and sides, and the child was supported in an immovable position by a grass pillow of frayed cedar bark, under the back of the neck.

The process commenced at birth and continued for eight to twelve months. Children cried when the board was removed, as they had become accustomed to the pressure. Flattening did not seem to affect their mental status in later years, according to statistics.

In the territory adjacent to the confluence of the Mississippi and Ohio rivers, however, we have found no trace of head flattening in our excavations during seven years, except a slight amount in the back, caused, no doubt, from the cradle board but not from using weights.

The image of a child or papoose strapped to a cradle board, extended on its back with seven bands holding it to the board, was reported by General Gates P. Thruston of Tennessee. Until recently there was no duplicate of this find when an almost exact copy was found in a stone box grave near Nashville, Tennessee.

The Mound Builder's forehead was low and receding, cheekbones high, and the maxillary region salient and ponderous. They had excellent teeth. One of our excavations showed eighteen teeth instead of the usual sixteen, with two pre-molars or bicuspids in the mandible, inside the regular line of teeth. Another mandible or lower jaw had a double impaction of the third molar, indicating that this individual had his two lower wisdom teeth on which he chewed turned sidewise, so he must have had the toothache all his life. We see, therefore, that the Mound Builder had trouble with his teeth, even as we have today. Generally speaking, however, his teeth were superior to ours today, for in our excavations, we find that the teeth are in fairly good condition.

According to Dr. Van Andrews of Cairo, Illinois, who has made a detailed examination of prehistoric skeletal material in Southern Illinois, Southeast Missouri, and Western Kentucky, his analysis shows that prehistoric man's teeth were about forty per cent better than our teeth.

On the other hand, Dr. W. D. Funkhouser of the University of Kentucky is of the opinion that "The teeth are, in general, in bad condition, worse than those of the average civilized man of today. In spite of the common notion to the contrary, it is evident that these primitive people had many and as varied troubles with their teeth as do the civilized races. Pathological conditions in the teeth are extremely common and represent most of the diseases and malformations found in modern man." [13]

The Indian blackened his teeth by chewing charred tobacco, and rubbed his teeth with the ashes of it every morning according to old records. Possibly the ashes of the tobacco helped preserve them.

Near the rivers, the Mound Builder had plenty of Vitamin D which, no doubt, had great effect on the dental structure before and after birth.

In conclusion, the early inhabitants of both Asia and America were almost identical in manners, customs, and physical appearance.

CHAPTER III

MOUNDS

JUST as today we have large cities, towns and hamlets, so in prehistoric times the Mound Builder had settlements of various sizes. Our forefathers emulated him in that they, also, preferred to build their cities on water, appreciating the fact that water afforded an easy means of transportation. Cincinnati, Columbus and Saint Louis formerly contained mounds, Saint Louis having been called the "Mound City."

The confluence of rivers, large and small, seemed to be a favorite building site for the Early Peoples. It was a natural stronghold for fortification, its isolated heights especially adapted for defense. By great labor and skill, earthworks, circular embankments of earth, with and without ditches, comparable to the moats one sees in Europe, along with enclosures from four to ten feet high, formed an impregnable line of defense from the enemy.

High places are beautiful and the Mound Builder loved beauty. This is demonstrated by their handsome ornaments, tools and pottery; and nothing can be compared to the magnificent sweep of great rivers and landscape in the distance from old high mound sites.

It almost seems as if the prehistoric peoples knew

the science of engineering and recognized some standard of measurement, as in the symmetrical enclosures
of the mounds are to be found squares, circles, ellipses,
and octagons with long connecting avenues which remind one of Avebury in England, Carnac in France, or
the Temples and Sphinx avenues of Egyptian Karnak
and Luxor. Some of the complicated approaches to
the earthworks are similar to Scottish hill forts. It is
amazing that people so partially civilized and crude
were able to construct squares, circles and other geo-
metrical figures on a scale which would tax the skill
of a well-trained engineer.

Protected by turf and interlaced roots of trees and
bushes, the humble mound bids defiance to the elements. Some are little changed; others are almost obliterated, and we don't know where to find them, even
from records. Our own forefathers, the pioneers of
American civilization, were too preoccupied with their
own problems of getting a living and pushing back
frontiers to worry about long-forgotten centuries. The
plow has obliterated many mounds and erosion and
rivers have claimed their share. The changing course
of rivers has revealed many artifacts in this country;
likewise in France, along the Somme, many artifacts
have been found.

Human labor lies behind most ancient monuments,
and mounds were built by loads of dirt, carried in a
skin or basket on the shoulders or in the arms of the
prehistoric peoples.

In the building of the Colosseum, Pyramids, Parthenon, Pantheon, the walls of Babylon, Peru, China, and Italy, gangs of slaves must have drawn the great stones to their places. The energy of man was the sole driving power.

In the British Museum, many of the wonderful bas reliefs depict prisoners and slaves in a chain gang, building pyramids and palaces. Some of the palaces had hundreds of richly decorated rooms. The ancients loved vastness and all things on a great scale.

The mounds in the Mississippi and Ohio Valleys, however, were not built by slaves, but with religious fervor, no doubt by the prehistoric peoples themselves.

There are two major cultural divisions in the Central Basin Area of the United States—Woodland and Mississippi. In the Woodland group, the mounds were usually for burial or ceremonial purposes, whereas in the Mississippi division mounds were generally constructed and served as bases for house sites, temple and council buildings and were usually truncated and pyramidal in form.

Among the largest mounds found are the great cone-shaped or conical mound at Miamisburg, Ohio, which was sixty-eight feet high and eight hundred fifty-two feet in circumference, when the first measurements were taken; the Grave Creek mound in Kenhawas, Virginia, seventy feet high and one thousand feet in circumference; the largest mound in the Etowah-Tomlin group at Cartersville, Georgia, which is sixty-six feet in height and almost three acres around the base; and the great truncated pyramid in Cahokia, two thousand feet in circumference, ninety feet high, and several acres in extent on the top. This is one of the largest earthworks in the world and is located at Collinsville, Illinois. It was called Monks Mound because at one time a colony of monks, known as the Trappists, had a monastery there. It is part of the group known as the Cahokia. To appreciate its size, one should climb to the top on a hot summer's day, as I did the first time I saw it.

Aerial explorations are revealing wonderful things to archæologists of the present day. Flights over Guatemala and Yucatan have revealed many ancient cities, hidden by the jungle. In Peru, a great wall, fifteen feet in height and width, was found, stretching inland from the coastal plains for forty miles. It was punctuated at intervals with forts of stone and adobe. Through aviation it was possible to make air maps of the vast ruins of Chanchan, in Peru, which cover eleven square miles. Air exploration is much superior to ground surveying where the large archæological sites are free of vegetation.

In this country, it is invaluable for photographing lines of fortification, moats and groups of mounds, especially those of the effigy type. When all the underbrush is cleared away and the grass mowed, small mounds appear that were never suspected, as has been

Water Spirit effigy on shore of Lake Koshkonong, Wisconsin

Turtle effigy mound, Lake Koshkonong, Wisconsin

One of the fifteen mounds at the King Site before excavation

A mound during excavation at the same site

Temple Mound, showing three clay altars and parts of two burned temple buildings at two levels

Tablet of King Mounds

Various buildings covering excavations

proven at the King Mounds. Several mounds have been added in this way.

There are more effigy mounds in Wisconsin than in any other part of the United States. These represent birds, animals, and even the human figure. In Dade County there is a human effigy that reminds one of a ginger-bread man.[14] He was one hundred and twenty-five feet from head to foot, with a measurement of one hundred and forty-five feet between the arms. It took immense time and labor to make these effigies.

Henry R. Schoolcraft suggests that the effigy mounds were totems and that the fox, bear, eagle, turtle, and other animals were the signs of various tribes. "A tribe could leave no more permanent trace of an esteemed Sachem or honored individual than by the erection of one of these monuments." [15] Excavations have shown that symbolical or effigy mounds reveal few relics.

Some of the effigy mounds are almost obliterated, the outline growing fainter each year. Accustomed to the large mounds of the Mississippi Valley, some of the effigy mounds in Wisconsin caused me to examine them very, very closely, for with some of them one needs a vivid imagination to see what one is supposed to see. However, on the shore of Lake Kashkonong, there are three fine effigies, one in the form of a turtle, another representing the Water Spirit effigy, and the third depicting a bird effigy.

Dr. Charles E. Brown, Director of the State Historical Society of Wisconsin, at Madison, and an authority on the aboriginal peoples of the Mississippi Valley states: "Present-day Wisconsin archæologists recognize the existence in the state of but two unquestioned man mounds, all others so described proving to be but bird effigies. The second mound of this character was located in the N. W. ¼ of Section 36, T. 13, R. 3 E., in Sauk County. It has been long obliterated." This remarkable mound lies on nearly level ground about 20 rods from the foot of a steep but talus-covered ridge. The legs are cut in two by the road at a point about 20 rods west of the Hoege school house, Joint District No. 9. Reference to the map will show that the mound is in the edge of a break in the bluffs which leads to the river some two miles distant. At present the head, arms and trunk are well preserved.

"Mr. William H. Canfield surveyed this mound in 1859. Cuts from his survey have appeared in various publications, and references to this mound are frequent. In several of these it is located wrongly. The mound lies with the head toward the south and the figure is in the attitude of walking toward the west." [16]

The effigy man mound at La Valle, Wisconsin, was destroyed years ago; the other is now preserved, thanks to the perseverance of Dr. Brown, in a state park near Baraboo, Wisconsin.

The serpent is symbolical in many countries and was especially venerated by the Mound Builder. One of the most impressive of effigy mounds is the Great Serpent mound in southern Ohio, situated between the Scioto and Miami Rivers. Conforming to the summit of the hill on which it is located, the body of the serpent in graceful undulations terminates with a triple coil at the tail. The figure is boldly defined, five feet high, a thirty-four feet base at the center of body, and about one thousand three hundred and thirty feet in length. The head has distended jaws as if in the act of swallowing what might be an egg one hundred and sixty feet in length. It is now the property of the Ohio Archæological and Historical Society, through the courtesy of the Peabody Museum of Harvard University. Authorities differ as to its being the largest and most impressive prehistoric effigy, as some claim the bird effigy in Eatonton, Georgia, is the finest effigy known. I would suggest a visit to both of them as they are worth seeing and are fine examples of prehistoric effigy tumuli in this country.

The Aztalan groups of mounds consist of seventeen acres on Rock River. The original large, square-terraced mounds are almost completely obliterated, but are being preserved by the State of Wisconsin. The most interesting find to me at Aztalan is the female burial with the shell beads.

Mound Building is not confined to the United States alone. Mounds are found in many other countries, although perhaps a better term is tumuli. They are known in Russia, Denmark, Sweden, Norway, England, and Italy. We have great shell mounds in Florida and California. They are also found in Scotland, Ireland, Brazil, Spain, Australia, Africa, and other parts of Europe. However, the shell heaps of this country reveal only Neolithic culture traits, while those of Europe show Azilian and Solutrean traits as well.[17]

The Mound Builder had no chimney.—"The chimney was unknown anywhere in the New World so when fires were built in the house the smoke escaped through the roof or the door." [18] When I made my first trip to Mexico and saw smoke pouring out of all the cracks, crevices, sides and roof of the buildings, I thought they were smoking tobacco as I had seen done so often in Kentucky. Instead, they were smoking the inhabitants of the home, because there was no chimney and the smoke had to escape somewhere. How fortunate we are to live in this age—no smoke to inflame one's eyes and no soot on the freshly washed linens.

Early archæologists were of the opinion that the larger the mound the more it would contain, but this has often been proved to the contrary. There is no way of determining what is in a mound except by opening it. As the population of the prehistoric cities has long since departed, the only method we have of determining the number that lived in any one place is by the quantity and size of their tumuli and by reading the kitchen midden. This may not be a true criterion, as certain groups may not have erected mounds in proportion to their number. However, the only method of determining the number is by what they left behind. From research and from our own excavations, and from work and investigations that have been made, we know the largest centers had the most tumuli.

The University of Illinois worked several seasons near Collinsville, Illinois, on the Cahokia groups of mounds, but the finds were very disappointing. On the other hand, the King Mounds at Wickliffe, Kentucky, have proven to be very rich. In seven years' work we have found that they yielded the greatest quantity of material and information about the aboriginal peoples of all mounds excavated to date in the United States. Up to January 1939, we have excavated 116,831 artifacts, all of which have been cleaned, marked and catalogued. I have washed more than thirty thousand potsherds and claim the woman's record for pot washing. There are records for steeple sitting, so why not a record for pot washing! However, to return to the subject, these were prehistoric sherds and pots and washing these discoveries is an invaluable way to study all prehistoric findings. I have much in common with Pandora, and am interested in seeing what is under the dirt accumulations of centuries.

None of us ever quite outgrows the lure of digging for buried treasure. Imagine the thrill of finding buried, deep in the earth on this continent, almost in the center of population, the thatched roof of a building which housed people centuries ago!

High overlooking the meeting of the Mississippi and Ohio Rivers, near Wickliffe, Kentucky, are some of the most interesting mounds in the Mississippi Valley, referred to above and known as the King Mounds. In a tract of virgin land, embracing twenty-five acres, are fifteen well defined mounds and a number of others, some scarcely perceptible. There is a line of fortifications protecting the natural approach from the Mississippi River to the bluff on which these early dwellers lived. The King Mounds are low, the highest being only twelve feet from the base. Meticulous care is taken to preserve everything, each element playing its part in helping to unravel the fabric of the story of the Mound Builder.

This site is unusual in that it shows a complete social unit like any city today, with buildings, dwellings, storage, and various other structures scattered here and there. There is a Council House comparable to a Courthouse, and Sweat-houses similar to a hospital unit. There is also the Temple or religious center, and the Burial Mounds.

Mounds are everywhere—simple, plane, truncated, terraced, pear-shaped, elliptical, square and pyramidal. They are generally made out of clay or whatever material was near by. Truncated mounds were used by the aborigines, as sub-structures for their temples and chief's dwellings. De Soto found that the historic Indians used the old mounds for the same purpose. Dr. John R. Swanton, chairman of the United States De

Soto Expedition Commission, has been making exten-
sive research, and it will be interesting to read his final
report.

CHAPTER IV

METHOD OF EXCAVATION

In the early excavations of the Mississippi Valley, very little effort was made to record the different shapes, sizes or locations of the mounds. Post-hole diggers and steel probes were often used to make tests. Consequently, much valuable material was ruined and missed.

Fortunately, careful archæologists soon learned that this method was unsatisfactory. There is only one proper way to open a mound and that is to excavate it throughout from end to end, or from side to side, to the undisturbed soil. In some cases, houses or barns have been erected on the top of mounds and then tunneling is employed. This method is being used in excavating Cholula in Mexico, as a church had been built on top of the pyramid.

Before any excavation starts, test pits are dug in various places to determine if the proposed site contains anything of archæological value, such as kitchen midden, potsherds and the like. Kitchen midden is always a pleasing sight to an archæologist, as it is in the stratified remains of refuse piles, debris or kitchen midden that we are able to piece together the actual living story of the struggle and cultural development of early peoples. Kitchen midden has been compared to a modern city dump, not very elegant to visualize, but a pre-historic "dump" is invaluable in rebuilding sequences of ancient history.

If the ground is not sterile, and the find seems a rich one, we employ what is called the five-foot method of excavating. In the meantime, if it is a mound, it has been surveyed and a contour map made. Then the surface to be excavated is staked off in five-foot squares, to facilitate measurements and the marking of objects uncovered. The lines used to govern the squares are designated by North, South, East, and West. The stakes are numbered 0, 5N, 10N, 15N, . . . 5S, 10S, 15S, . . . 5E, 10E, 15E, . . . 5W, 10W, 15W, . . . and can be expanded indefinitely.

For example, from the square of a mound, marked fifteen feet East, and ten feet North from the zero mark, each piece of material found bears the number 15E, 10N, meaning that the material was excavated from fifteen feet East, and ten feet North of its beginning point, or 0. The artifact also carries another mark to indicate the depth of the find. Materials found in each twelve-inch level are kept separate and bear notations of first, second, third, or fourth level, denoting the depth from the surface of the mound.

Where sites are scattered, often the county or state numerals are used, but when work is concentrated at one particular site, or where there are a number of mounds, each mound is labeled Mound A, Mound B, Mound C, etc. A pottery bowl found in the King

[33]

Mounds with the inscription "45E, 15N, 3L, MD" would indicate that the artifact came from the ninth square, or forty-five feet east from the point of beginning; three squares or fifteen feet north from the starting point; thirty-six inches below the surface of the mound, or in the third twelve-inch level; and was found in the fourth mound excavated, or Mound D.

It is by reading these inscriptions, which are marked with indelible ink, that any student or archæologist can locate the exact five-foot square where the material was found, an invaluable record for future generations.

The top soil or sod is removed a few feet ahead of the worker. Generally a six-inch level, or the depth of a spade, represents the first removal of soil. The dirt is thrown well back of the dig, and before it is taken away the loose dirt is carefully sifted. Should the archæologist have overlooked any small object such as beads, or fine bone needles, for example, these will be recovered. Many of the finest specimens of the art of the Mound Builder have been rescued from these screens or sieves.

To make a neat job, care must be taken to keep the vertical face as smooth and straight as possible. Each profile is carefully studied, as stratigraphy plays an important part in archæology. The method of horizontal and vertical excavating enables one to detect easily any signs of kitchen midden, post molds, fire pits, outlines of buildings, and charcoal, which at the King Mounds is invariably indicative of burials. However,

Colonel and Mrs. King, with associates, at the King Mounds

charcoal is also found in burned buildings and fire pits.

If the weather is warm, a canvas is erected to keep the sun off the workers; but here at the King Mounds, possibly because of the close proximity to the rivers, there is generally a cool breeze to fan weary brows. Excavating requires infinite care and patience; it is slow and tedious work, and very often aching backs result from such constant stooping. It is fascinating, however, for one never knows what the newly excavated earth will reveal. Some days nothing at all; other days, perhaps a beautiful pendant, some fine flint, a broken piece of shell, a pottery sherd, a bead, or the actual remains of a people who lived in a thriving city long ago. It is the fascination of the unknown which attracts us. There is a constant lure comparable, no doubt, to the urge of gold miners and explorers.

Each day a record is kept of the finds and, if important, photographs are taken showing the position and relation of objects. Otherwise, illustrations are made by hand in the field notebook. A large paper bag is marked as to level and square, and whatever is excavated there is placed in the bag. Hundreds of bags are used and all are carefully marked, so that when the contents are washed or brushed these also can be marked. In this way, when the excavation is completed, every piece can be identified as to place of recovery. Burials are left *in situ,* and post molds, fire pits, and everything of like character are left undisturbed, so that the story can be read.

Excavations move rapidly when the mounds are sterile, but many weeks are consumed if the find is rich. In an area covering forty by eighty feet, in one of the King Mounds, sixty thousand pieces were excavated at an average depth of four feet. The material was highly concentrated and required careful and expert work. Twelve thousand cubic feet of dirt were taken from the Temple Mound alone and it is only one-twentieth excavated.

When anything is located in the dirt, camel's hair brushes are used to brush away the earth, and with the aid of an orange-wood stick, similar to that used by manicurists, the packed soil is loosened. Utmost precaution must be observed at this stage of the excavation not to break the artifact, sherd, pot, or whatever appears.

A bricklayer's small trowel is often used to advantage. Before these are used, however, we round off the sharp point with a file, so that there will be no danger of scratching the artifact. Orange-wood sticks are most satisfactory, because they are strong and do not scratch fragile surfaces. We were presented with a set of digging tools made out of hickory wood, which are most effective. Hickory is a tough wood, and when steamed can be bent to any desired shape, which is retained when dry. These hickory chisels, awls, and spatulas closely resemble the bone tools of the Mound Builder.

The prehistoric Indians made and used great quantities of pottery; consequently, more pieces of pottery are found than any other material. In uncovering a piece of pottery, a rim may be discovered first, and one immediately visualizes an entire pot, only to find that it is but a portion, as entire pots seldom occur. One always hopes that something valuable may be found. An air of expectancy prevails with each member of an archæological organization.

Sometimes we become so interested in the excavation that we don't want to stop work. Many times, both Colonel King and myself dig until sun-down, especially if an interesting floor, building, or artifact takes an outline.

Caches are wonderfully interesting to me for they represent the work of an individual, and are usually beautifully made. A cache may consist of beads, pottery, flints and bone implements.

The wealth of material in the ground here is amazing, all due to the fact that the site was undisturbed by the plow, and on studying and reading the kitchen midden, we know that groups of aborigines lived here continuously for several hundred years.

With many burials, pottery bowls with mussel shells are found near the head and feet, food provisions, no doubt, for the long journey into the unknown. Ornaments are uncovered around the neck, wrists and ankles. Occasionally a flint dagger or a spear point is found near the right forearm. However, on the whole, very few war-like implements have been excavated, and the deduction is that the Mound Builders evidently were a peaceful, agricultural, sedentary, and religious group. Often a cache of objects is found at the hands or feet. There is no set method in the placing of these objects. Extreme care must be taken in the uncovering in order that each grain of evidence may be preserved and allowed to remain *in situ*. The skeletal material is especially well preserved at Wickliffe, because the mounds were built on high places, and charcoal was placed over and under the burials, neutralizing the acids of the earth.

Mussel shells are very fragile and crumble easily when excavated. Skeletal material found in damp places is often quite soft, and frequently it is necessary to apply a thin coating of acetone and ambroid to preserve it. Both shell and bone are composed principally of lime, which hardens when it is dry.

The contents of each marked bag are carefully washed, sorted and marked. Any perishable objects, such as partially disintegrated mussel shell, ornaments and botanical substances that might be harmed by washing, are brushed. Experience teaches one which kind of brush to use, and usually ordinary tooth brushes suffice.

In sorting the material from the dig, pottery is separated into various colors, and the decorated and plain sherds are put by themselves, as well as the rims and handles. Shells and animal and fish bones are classified. Corn, beans, and nuts are carefully examined and fre-

[38]

quently coated with ambroid to preserve them. In many instances, pieces of fabric and corn caches are left in the matrix, so one is able to see the undisturbed earth and contents. There are many classifications; for example, with deer bones alone, there are approximately twenty-five separate divisions. This is equally true with other artifacts.

Before the excavated material is placed in cases for display and study, each piece must be handled more than thirty times by various members of an archæological staff. Then it is ready for specialization. As an illustration, shells must be classified by a person who, through long years of experience, has devoted his life to the study of mollusks. A lithic expert must make his report on the rocks and flints. The ceramic specialist must study and report on the sherds or broken bits of pottery. The botanical finds are arranged for the palæobotanist to study. A mineralogist must identify the lead, copper and other minerals. An ichthyologist and zoologist must study and examine fish and fowl bones for special reports. We even require a criminologist, as finger prints of the Mound Builder have been left on pottery and pieces of clay wattle. Everything has to be carefully recorded and preserved for future study.

Through the brilliant work of Dr. A. E. Douglas, it is possible to date ruins by dendrochronology, or the study of tree rings. One of his workers did research on the charred timbers at the King Mounds in 1934, and eventually we hope to be able to know the exact date of the mounds.

Dr. A. T. Erwin, an authority on maize and cucurbits, or a study of the squash family, spent several days here studying the maize. Four great caches have been excavated at the King Mounds. Small quantities of scattered grain and cobs have been prevalent in all the excavations, a particularly large cache having been found in Mound E, which really was a village site. Dr. Erwin reported orally that the maize is the most primitive that he has seen in the Mississippi Valley. The cobs are so small that many of the ears contain only six rows of grain.

The duty of all earnest archæologists is to remove the material from the ground in an orderly, scientific manner; record the finds, preserve the material, and deliver it to the specialist in his particular field in such perfect condition that the findings will add conclusively to our knowledge of the Mound Builder who lived in this country, long before Columbus discovered America.

CHAPTER V

MOUND CONTENTS AND BURIALS

MANKIND the world over believes in some kind of life after death. It seems to be inherent in the human race. There is, however, a wide difference in views of Eternity.

Most of us today believe in a spiritual hereafter. But we do not bury personal belongings with our dead, as we believe that only the spirit lives. Many highly developed groups, the Egyptians, for instance, believed with our prehistoric groups in a material hereafter. Fortunately for archæology, the first inhabitants of the Mississippi Valley that preceded the historic Indian held the belief that their actual possessions, ornaments, and tools would be used in the next life. And it is in the tombs and burials that we learn the greatest part of their story.

At the King Mounds there are three types of burials —prone or dorsal, basket burials, and cremation.

The prone or dorsal burial was full length, as we bury our dead. Basket or bundle burial was used in many lands. The body was originally placed elsewhere, probably on a platform beyond the reach of dogs, wolves and other preying animals. The flesh was removed by insects and birds, and later, when only the bones remained, they were carefully collected in a bundle or basket and reburied.

Another illustration of the bundle burial is the death of a relative or friend away from home who is brought back for interment. This occurred often with the prehistoric races, and the only method possible of returning the body was by bundle burial.

Cremation was practiced extensively by the Mound Builder. During the process, many perishable articles were consumed, no doubt. In some of the premeditated burnings, or sacrificial fires, bones are found intermingled with the charcoal, stone implements, and other evidences of sacrifices and tribute to the deceased.

Many Christians wished to be buried in Jerusalem, as it is the center of the Christian religion. Other creeds have their great centers, such as Mecca of the Mohammedans. From the great number of burials here at the King Mounds, this must have been a religious center where the prehistoric Indians wished to be buried. The Burial Mound contains one hundred and fifty-three burials of three distinct types: bundle or reburial, extended dorsal, and cremated. The bodies were buried with their favorite pottery, tools, fine flints, bone implements, and jewelry. They were placed on the ground, rather than in it, the surface soil being scraped away slightly, and the body covered to a depth of one or more feet. A very fortunate circumstance was the mixture of charcoal in the burials, for this neutralized the acid condition of the soil and preserved the skeletal material. One wonders if the burials were placed upon beds of hot coals, as there is every evidence throughout the entire excavation that they were fire worshipers.

All ages are represented. Longevity, however, seems to be the exception, only one individual reaching the age of sixty years or more. This woman had lost all her teeth prior to death, as her teeth sockets had filled in completely with bone.

In the center of the mound lie the remains of a male with a skull trophy between his feet. In life he must have been of elevated rank, as two large earrings carved from wood and covered with a thin plating of beaten copper were found near his head. These rings encircle seven pointed stars and are beautifully preserved by the metallic salts caused by the oxidation of the copper.

Compared to our present racial standards, these people were rather short in stature. The pottery-maker was barely four feet in height. She lies buried with her six various-sized, mushroom-shaped trowels, made of pottery clay, a piece of round-edged gravel for making incised lines and a piece of cannel coal at her head. As no other pottery trowels were found, it is evident that she was the pottery-maker for the community.

In another section of the Burial Mound are the remains of a man who was an artisan of another type. Perhaps he was the leather worker, for close to his side are his tools—bone implements consisting of needles, skivers, awls, spatulas and scrapers, some made from fish spines, others from bone of deer and wild turkey. Near him is a family group, father, mother, and baby clasped closely in the mother's arm.

Many effigy types of vessels were found, representing the human figure, animals and birds. One of the handsomest is a painted water bottle, made in the shape of an owl resting on the two feet and the tip of the tail. Another artistic bowl is formed in the shape of a plumed eagle, all filled, no doubt, with provisions for the great journey into the Unknown, according to the rites consecrated by usage or superstition.

One man was found buried face down with a rock on his head. He evidently was in some disgrace.

Orientation of the skeletal material indicates that all were buried facing the sun. They radiate in a semi-circle, evidently following the course of the sun during the season. Reading the shadows, most of them were buried around nine o'clock in the morning. No burial has been found that does not follow the orientation, with the exception of the infants, who are buried indiscriminately under the floors of the homes.

Mound D, the fourth mound to be excavated of the twenty which comprise the group of the King Mounds, has been recently completed. Obviously, this last mound is the children's mound, for at its base sixty-three infants were found. They are *in situ*. There was no set method in their burials, as some are on their backs and others on their sides, with their feet crossed. Some face each other, perhaps in a twin burial; others have their little knees up to their chins in a flexed or prenatal burial. One infant had a string of shell beads around its neck and near the hand of another lay a beautifully carved white bone doll, three inches in length; another had a miniature clay doll; another a tiny clay bear. Others were surrounded by tiny, three legged bowls, one with a snake head for a handle, another in the shape of a small hand, and others in the shape of fish and animals—all telling a simple, poignant story of paternal love and devotion. One thing apparently that has never changed all through the ages is a parent's love. The Infant Mound, or Mound D, is a miniature of the adult burial mound, for the children, too, lie surrounded by their chosen possessions.

Catlin describes the Mandans as placing skulls of their dead in a circle. Each wife knew the skull of her former husband or child and visited them each day, bringing a dish of the best cooked food, chatting to them as if they were alive!

Recently we excavated a number of skulls arranged in an elongated circle. In the center and between the skulls were tool sharpeners, pottery, paint stone, and other offerings. The clay under the offerings was burned to a bright red color, to a depth of three inches. This was, no doubt, a ceremonial burial altar.

In Europe, during the Transitional Azilian and Tardenoisian epochs of the Neolithic and Paleolithic, or old and new Stone Ages, oftentimes groups of skulls were found in caves associated with bright red ocher and offerings. There was no association of ideas or connections between these burials and the former, but both embrace similar thought.

Fire played an important part in the burials. It is apparent in those we have excavated that the charcoal was either prepared ahead of time, or the fire was allowed to burn only a short while before the blaze quenched by heaping earth over it. Charcoal is found under and above the skeletal material and the bones are unaffected by fire.

Few weapons were found in the burials that we have excavated. Instead, ornaments, beads of bone and shell, flints and pottery are found. Sometimes mica was placed around the body, occasionally in the form of figures, discs, ovals and curves.

In Grave Creek Mound, overlooking the conjunction of Grave Creek and the Ohio River, a shaft was sunk in 1838 which disclosed two chambers made of logs. The first tomb held three skeletons and four thousand shell beads, ornaments of mica, a copper bracelet and a stone disc. In the lower tomb were ten skeletons, in sitting positions. It was indicative of human sacrifice that they had been buried with a distinguished chief or shaman.

It has been suggested, when great quantities of beads are found in burials, that instead of being ornaments they represented the man's record of achievements, his scroll of fame, as it were; he might have been some great sachem whose wisdom and sagacity had saved his people from the enemy.

Man was forced at an early era to know surgery. Several examples of the delicate operation of trepanation have been found in prehistoric man burials.

Mound D at the King Mounds is rectangular in shape and measures one hundred and five feet by fifty-five feet. Its greatest height is six feet. It presents a very vivid picture of the living conditions of ancient peoples. The mound itself is built over many building sites, as indicated by various outlines, all large and rectangular in shape, with the exception of one circular structure, twenty-two feet in diameter. This structure no doubt had some religious significance and was perhaps the sacred precinct of the shaman, or medicine man, as nothing was found inside, no evidence of fire or kitchen midden. It seems to have been kept purposely clean. One learns from literature pertaining to the prehistoric peoples that ceremonialism was developed to an unusual degree, and the shaman occupied an important place. This round structure might have been a place where grain was stored, or a treasure house similar to those of the historic Indian.

"Powhatan had a treasure house, fifty by sixty yards in length, frequented only by priests, where he kept his valuables, such as skins, beads, pearls and copper, stored up against the time of his death and burial. Here also was his store of red paint for ornaments, bows and arrows, shields and clubs. At the corners of the house stood four images as sentinels, one a dragon, another a bear, the third like a leopard, and the fourth like a giant man, made 'evill favoredly according to their best workmanship.' " [19]

The Council House mound is rectangular in shape, measuring twenty-one by twenty-five feet. It contains three fire pits with the white ashes of the ceremonial fires still remaining, which must have blazed in rituals centuries ago. There is a gap in the wall indicative of a doorway. Within the dwelling are post molds, placed about ten inches apart, suggestive of a platform for a shaman and his audience. Near the post molds is the outline of a building, surrounded by a prehistoric drainage ditch. In this building were found seven pieces of pottery graduated in size. All have two or more handles, with the exception of one small, smooth black bowl, which has a fluted rim. Four of the larger bowls have a red ocher lining. Near the pottery were charred maize cobs, a bone turkey-caller made from a leg of a wild turkey, a rectangular piece of polished purple fluorspar, two flat discs made from pottery clay, and a large ring of cannel coal which was probably used as a hair ornament.

The Temple Mound is the largest and highest mound in the King group and commands a superb view of the Ohio and Mississippi Rivers for many miles. It is devoted to religion. In this mound are three rectangular clay altars, carrying out the trinity idea that is found in both the Burial and Council House Mounds. This has caused much speculation, as the trinity occurs in

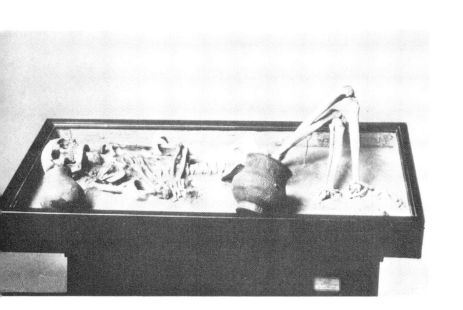

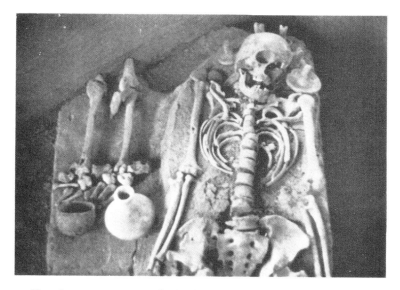

Showing contrasts and similarities between burials and potteries in Neolithic Period, Germany (upper) and King Mounds, Kentucky (lower). Plate 1, Courtesy of Berlin Museum; plate 2, Courtesy of R. R. Evans, Indianapolis, Ind.

Infant burials with dolls and rattles: front and side view of doll
excavated with infant at the King Mounds

Excavating a Mound

Burial Tombs at the Ancient Buried City, Wickliffe, Kentucky

many different religions. Indications point to the worship of three different deities or different religious customs, each altar being dedicated perhaps to the worship of some one deity and burnt offerings made according to the religious customs of the ancient peoples. These offerings may have been food, articles of adornment, or living animal sacrifices, as is evidenced by a charred rope found near the altar. However, this is all conjecture.

In front of the altars are post molds, indicating a prayer rail where the supplicants knelt in devotion to their gods. Concrete evidence of two burned buildings has been found with portions of the thatched roofs composed of split canes and grass, charred timbers and the blackened rope mentioned above. Evidently these superimposed buildings were burned to appease the anger of some god, for if they had been burned by accident the ashes would have been removed. But there were no ashes! Instead, the collapsed building was covered with earth while burning and then rebuilt at a higher level, so we know that the burning was premeditated, another indication of fire worship.

At the base of Mound D, the outlines of six small buildings, with post molds at regular intervals, were found. Split cane was woven between the posts like a wicker chair, and clay, mixed with water and grass and forming a clay wattle, plastered the building. They were subjected to fire, both inside and out, as the walls show evidence of violent heat. They may have been pottery kilns or used for sweat-houses, like our modern Turkish baths, since this was a center of living. As we have previously excavated the Temple Mound, the Council House Mound and the Adult Burial Mound, perhaps it was used as a spa, like Hot Springs, or various watering places in this country and abroad, such as in Finland, where it is customary to have thermal baths once or twice a week, the sweathouse oftentimes being built before the house or barn is completed.

In the middle of one of the structural outlines, three feet from the base of the mound, two adult extended burials were found completely covered with cypress and other wood bark. We also found a burial pit, the bottom covered by stones and six bundle burials.

One altar was found with a path of post molds on either side, leading to it. No ashes were found, so it might have been a place where offerings of flowers were made; or, again, it might have been a work table. All this is conjecture, however, until the entire story of prehistoric man is completed.

The great accumulation of kitchen midden proves convincingly that this mound was built in a slow and gradual manner and that a large number of people lived here at one time. In the kitchen debris literally thousands of broken sherds, discarded bone implements, and other miscellaneous material have been found. So much kitchen midden caused the soil to become very black from decomposition.

Five fire pits were found. One, raised and concave,

two feet in diameter, shows evidence of great heat, as it has a layer of fire-hardened clay baked almost to a brick.

With the American aborigines the house for a single family was the exception; houses large enough for several families were the rule, somewhat like our tenement houses or our early apartment buildings.

All of the buildings we have excavated are of the small pole or timber construction, the post holes not being larger than six or seven inches in diameter. Major William S. Webb reports that he found in Eastern Tennessee two types of constructions used in the buildings excavated, "large log" and "small log." [20] These are indicative of two groups having lived there at different times. Major Webb's excellent work, with the able assistance of Prof. T. M. N. Lewis, Head of the Department of Anthropology, University of Tennessee, has added significantly to our knowledge of the Norris Basin region.

Some people do not approve of archæology, nor believe that it is adding to our knowledge of man, but feel like the woman who lived near Dayton, Tennessee, where the famous Scopes trial was held. She came to see our excavations. When Colonel King inquired what she thought of them, she was most indignant and replied, "It is sacrilegious and agin religion." "Why?" he asked. She answered, "To bother these people who have been dead so long and uncover them to everybody's view." The Colonel had a happy inspiration and

[51]

asked if she believed in the Judgment Day when we all hope to arise and walk again. She immediately answered, "Why they is all ready—no dirt on 'em, and I don't live far from here." And she went away a convert to archæology.

Another time, in the first year of excavations at the King Mounds, in the midst of intense work, a group of men and women came to see the work, sunbonnets and overalls predominating. The leader of the group said, "I can tell you when them folks was buried and all about 'em."

Immediately we were all attention, since that is the subject archæologists, ethnologists, dendrochronologists, geologists and all the 'ologists have been trying to determine. With one accord we said, "When?" "Back in the years when they was puttin' the railroad through here, they had the 'cholery' and all them folks was buried." I had just finished excavating a beautiful pottery bowl and I said, "How do you account for the bowl being buried with this person and no fillings in the teeth, or buttons, or any indications of recent burials?" "Well," he replied, "I don't know, but that's my story and I'se going to stick to it." And even to this day, many of the natives do stick to it, and the old story recurs every so often, with the exception that sometimes the disease changes from "cholery" to yellow fever during the Civil War, and then we are excavating victims of yellow fever on "Dead Man's Hill."

The historic Indian loved pomp and ceremony.

MOUND CONTENTS AND BURIALS

When De Soto in 1540 paid his respects to Tuscaluza, the temple of Natchez was located on a truncated mound, with steps of gradual ascent. The great chief sat on a pile of cushions, while his attendants stood around awaiting his commands, one holding a colored shield to screen him from the sun. If the chief sneezed, everyone present was supposed to bow his head and say, "The sun preserve you—the sun make you great." The chief had great authority and his people paid him their complete homage. At his death women and children were buried with him, comparable to the burial customs of the prehistoric groups.

Mounds were a protection against floods. Some of the first of man's dwellings were made on poles, such as the famous Swiss Lake Dwellers. Similar structures are to be seen in the Pacific Islands, on the Amazon and Po Rivers, and in various parts of Mexico. With them have been found implements of the early and late Stone Ages, the Bronze and Copper Ages.

It is said that the traditional name of ancient mounds among the Choctaw Indians was "Nanne-yah," or the "Hills or Mounts of God." The historic Indian had great respect for the ancient mounds of his forefathers, and they were only occasionally disturbed for intrusive burials.

An interesting burial of the historic Indian was that of Black Bird, great chief of the Omahas. When his intuition told him to prepare for the long journey to the "Happy Hunting Grounds," like Jacob of Bib-

[53]

lical times, he gave instructions for his burial. He ordered that his most beautiful robes, with beads and scalps hanging, be placed upon his body, along with his great eagle-plumed headdress. A well-filled tobacco pouch was to be put in his hand to sustain him until he reached the land of his fathers. He had a favorite white horse on which he wished to be seated, wrapped in finely woven blankets. He chose as his last resting place the loftiest bluff on the Missouri River, where he could see the great water stretching into the distance. Medicine men and the sorrowing clan performed the great fire ceremony, after which a cedar post was erected to mark the hallowed spot. Such grave poles are found in Alaska, Chile, and other countries.

One of the greatest of all mounds or pyramids is in Cholula, on the way to Pueblo in Mexico. It is two hundred feet high and is larger in diameter than any of the Egyptian Pyramids. We were very much interested in seeing the first excavations made at the base of the pyramid, so we went with the man in charge of excavations way down under the earth. It was necessary to carry candles, and mine always went out in the darkest and narrowest passages. I was very glad to get out into the sunlight again.

Señor Javier Romero has recently published, *Estudio de los Entierros de la Piramide de Cholula, A Study of the Interior of the Pyramid of Cholula.* There were thirty-one burials, scattered in various parts, ranging in age from seven to seventy. In one burial shown, a hole was left in the tomb, in order that the spirit might escape. Most of them were in a sitting position, legs flexed as in prenatal burial.

Some beautiful pottery sherds of brilliant color and design were found, as well as ornaments and bone implements. In one of the burials, a bone flute was excavated, which is in excellent condition. In Neolithic times use was made of the bone flute. In a Pile village in Concise, Switzerland, a bone flute was found which had three holes, one for the mouth and two for the fingers. Bone and stone flutes have been excavated in Kentucky mounds. In Ecuador bone flutes and shell trumpets were found; while in Costa Rica and Peru stone and wooden flutes were used, and whistles were made from pottery in the shape of birds, similar to the Mound Builder's bird stones. Prehistoric peoples had the drum, rattle, and the flute, so all races have had chants or music of some kind.

Many composers such as Cadman, Coleridge Taylor, Lieurance, Logan and others have woven the tribal melodies of the Indian and his flute into beautiful themes, some, no doubt, having been handed down for generations.

In Mexico, Quetsalcotl, milder god of the Aztecs, was venerated as the divine teacher of peace. Fruits and flowers in season were used as offerings to his worship. His reign was known as the "golden age" in Mexico, because he taught the people agriculture, metallurgy and the art of government. The great pyramid Cholula was reared and dedicated to his worship. For twenty years he remained, teaching the people the art of civilization, and then sailed away in a vessel made out of a serpent's skin. Tradition lived on that the bark of the great Deity would revisit their shores. When the Spaniards first visited the holy city, his image occupied a shrine on the summit and an undying flame flung its radiance far into the night to keep alive the memory of the good Deity who would return and restore the "golden age." The Indians had such faith that he would return, that before they realized the Spaniards were their enemies, they confused them with the return of their great god.

A descendant of the Indian told me that the Indians have hidden their gods and idols in the altars of the cathedrals so they can worship the gods of their fathers when they go to church. Guadalupe is a favorite church of the Indian and of all the cathedrals in Mexico, it is one of the few that has never been fired upon in the many revolutions. The natives keep the beautiful silver altar covered with thousands of fresh flowers.

The Ohio Valley had a special attraction for the Mound Builder. Literally thousands of mounds have been found in the State of Ohio alone. In one mound, nineteen inches from the surface, a smooth level floor of burned clay was found on which a layer of sand had been spread. On this were plates of mica, overlapping like fish scales in an area twenty by five feet. Other mounds, especially those of the Fort Ancient and

Hopewell Culture, had beautiful ornaments of shell and copper. In Adams County eighteen circular plates of shell, thirteen of which had the design of a rattlesnake, were found. Others report coiled serpents of carved stone, carefully enveloped in sheet mica and copper.

The use of shell interests me. Borrowed usages help the ethnologist track "footprints of migrating nations to their earlier home." We have found large marine shells in the burials, and instead of their being hoes I feel that they had some other significance, similar to that predominating in other countries, where large shells are rare and costly offerings in honor of the dead. In India, China and Siam, they are prized by the natives; they are venerated to such an extent in China that great prizes are given for them. In the British Museum one may see fine examples. The Emperor of China is anointed with consecrated oil, at his coronation, held in one of these large shells. Sometimes the shaman administered medicine out of them. Some are elaborately carved.

There are many methods of communication in the present day—telegraph, telephone, wireless and the radio. The prehistoric groups living in the Mississippi Valley had an entirely different means of communication. They used smoke signals, and by a series of signal mounds, complete communication for hundreds of miles could be transmitted.

Mound F of the King Mounds is in the third year of

excavation and will be completed this year. It is eighty by forty feet and was originally a small, cone-shaped emplacement on an elongated mound. On this mound was stationed the lookout for protection against enemy attack, to warn of enemy approach and announce the return of tribes and visitors. Prehistoric signal fire ashes, layer upon layer, reveal fires which sent smoke signals with rapidity up and down the Mississippi and Ohio Rivers, hundreds of years ago. Remains of house sites were found, and a fire pit near which there was a charred basket and parts of thirty fish of various kinds, although only the bony parts, such as the fins, scales and vertebrae remained. As in the Infant Mound, we are excavating many children ranging in age from premature to two years. Small pots, mussel shells for food, and pebbles and pottery trowels are being found with them. Paternal love is something that doesn't change all through the ages.

I was interested in the wrappings of a female mummy in Peru, who had the locks of her living relatives to take along with her on her journey; also her needle of thorn near her weaving. A little infant was buried with her and enveloped in a black cloth, carefully wrapped and then enclosed in a penguin skin with the feathered side inward. The head was covered with a cap, lined with human hair, no doubt the mother's, and colored with red pigment. A pair of little sandals about three and one half inches long was fastened to a small woolen wrapper. The umbilical cord with seven knots, according to custom, was in an envelope of skin.

All primitive earthworks have something in common. This is especially true of contents and burials in the mounds where we find the art and customs of the ancient peoples.

CHAPTER VI

CLOTHING

I HAVE written to many scientists for their idea on the clothing of the Mound Builder. Although I have excavated fabric and other material and have considerable knowledge along these lines, I couldn't seem to visualize the figure of a stream-lined flapper of the Mound Builder period, standing tip-toe atop the Temple Mound, watching the sun set over the great rivers.

One witty scientist replied, "No wonder! I don't think she wore much." Another said, "That was about all she had—a figure." So the flapper of the Mound Builder was almost entirely stream-lined, or practically nude on the river bank, instead of "on the ranch."

No one has ever seen the complete dress of a Mound Builder, male or female, because most of the perishable garments of these people deteriorated long before Columbus discovered America.

As the historic Indian group followed the Mound Builder in occupancy of the great river basin, we must, of necessity, borrow from them and other aboriginal groups where data and information coincide. To quote Dr. Clark Wissler: "Yet even in exceptional cases where an abundance of materials is accidentally procured, or revealed by the unusual skill of the excavator, the outline of the culture is still so incomplete that the imagination must be called into play to fill out the picture. In consequence, a large part of the archæological writing is occupied with reading community life into the meager data. At best, such interpretations must be inferential and imaginative, or at least based upon circumstantial evidence; though for all that they are not to be dismissed lightly, because if properly checked by verifiable data for living peoples, they possess high degrees of probability."

Old prints of Du Pratz, drawings of DeBatz, and the figurines of terra cotta excavated from the Turner group of mounds in Ohio indicate that men wore a breech clout, and women a little apron made out of the inside bark of trees or skins of animals. The women's aprons were longer in the back than the breech clout for the men.[21]

From Jesuit records and other early writers we find, "In summer they go naked having only the private parts covered with a patch." . . . "the common sort have scarce to cover their nakedness, but with grasse, the leaves of trees or such like." [22] "The men have their secrets hid with a deer's skin." [23] And in 1744 Charlevoix wrote, "They used shells to cover their nakedness like our first parents did fig leaves."

In southern countries, where the hanging moss was prevalent, a bit of moss was used as Eve wore her fig leaf. Often the hanging moss in Florida is a little depressive, but it was useful to the prehistoric southern groups. Modesty was much more essential to them than to the harmless little cherubs one sees in the Vatican at Rome who are almost weighed down with their added voluminous fig leaves.

The Mound Builder, like most prehistoric inhabitants, was an artist at tanning and dressing hides. The hair was removed from the skin and it was scraped to the desired thickness, then rubbed. By the addition of oil to the animal hides and with slow tanning over fires, some of the skins were made as soft as velvet. Very often the skins were painted various colors and done so perfectly that, for example, a colored red hide looked as if it were red velvet. Skins of animals, like deer and bear, were tanned by placing the leather for an hour or more into boiling dye made from the bark of trees. This made the hide impervious to water and dirt.

Sometimes a deer skin was fastened to the shoulder, extending halfway down the leg, the bottom of which was cut into strips for fringe. It was fastened around the waist by a sash or snake skin. All the rest of the body was naked. Usually, even with a cape, one of the shoulders and breasts was left bare. Mantles or blankets were also made out of squirrel pelts, the tails being used for fringe.

These ancient peoples used the skins of rabbit, muskrat, opossum, deer, bear, fox and beaver for capes and blankets. Small animal skins were sometimes worn between the legs and twisted around the waist. The shirt or jacket, made without arms from bear or deer skins, as worn by the historic Indians, comes down, no doubt, through the ages from the prehistoric Indian. The head and skin of the mallard duck, with its beautiful iridescent feathers, were sewn together with thread made from deer sinew or grasses and used for capes and headdresses. Sometimes cane sticks were covered with many feathers, forming a smooth, colorful ceremonial wand used by the shaman.

The Mound Builder went barefoot, or wore sandals made from the skin of animals or fiber fabric from the inner bark of trees or cattail plants. Many similar sandals of the prehistoric peoples are found in dry caves today. In winter, close-fitting leggings of tanned deer skin were worn.

Little children wore practically nothing. Babies were carried in baskets or wicker boards on their mother's back, strapped from the head. A board was made of pleated willow on which a buckskin cloth was attached to form a pouch or sack. In winter, some animal fur, such as wild cat, was used for warmth.

Wild hemp or grasses were steeped, then beaten, and made into fabric. Fabric was also made from the inner bark of the mulberry tree, twisted in double thread, similar to our burlap or gunny sack. A rectangular piece was brought around the waist to the knees, forming a slit skirt for the female. Some historic Indians used to pleat corn leaves for various uses, similar in construction to the shuck mats of our forefathers, which are in evidence before many doors in reconstructed Williamsburg, Virginia, today.

We have excavated many colors of ocher—black, white, gray, and many beautiful shades of brown, yellow, and red, the red shading from pink to the deepest maroon in color. Last year I excavated a large piece of ocher and one of white, which represented quite a bank account to the prehistoric inhabitant to which it belonged, as ocher was used to paint the body and hair for everyday use, for ceremonials, and for burials. In burials, sometimes the face was painted black and the remaining part of the body red. Ocher was used along with vegetable dyes in coloring fabrics and pottery. It was used also to paint the body in different stripes and designs, such as birds and figures, and was a way of expressing their art, a sort of pictograph on the skin, as it were, with only themselves to interpret the meaning. They painted their faces something like the faces of clowns in the circus. Sometimes the lids of the eye, eyebrow, and cheek were painted black, the balance of the face red and blue, with small stripes on the cheek.

The Mound Builder had both mineral paint and vegetable dye and mixed them with water and with oil made from nuts, sunflowers, and animal fat. According to Father Marquette, the earth itself was of various colors and, mixed with fats, served as a potent dye. Near Columbus, Kentucky, he found purple, violet, and red earth being used by the natives for personal adornment and other purposes.

Figurines of pottery showing hair-dress—(1) Knot on top of head; (2) At base; (3) Peruke type; (4) Front-view on brow; (5) Hair piled on top and divided into knots. All excavated from the King Mounds

Heads excavated at the same location on the King Mounds, probably made by the same person. Note hair in piles or knots on top of head.

Human effigy types of pottery—(1) Figure on knees, hair combed back from brow; (2) Female figure with head-dress, breasts and arms decorated with black paint, body painted red, face light-colored slip or paint. Henderson Kentucky Excavations. (3) Female figure—note position of hands. (All in the King Collection)

Hands made of pottery. A great number of these were found in the various excavations at the King Mounds

The root, bark, and berries of the sumac were used. The bark and berries made a dark solution and the roots made a red dye. Sumac also had medicinal qualities, and it can be said with certainty that since the coming of the Europeans to this continent they have not added or discovered any economic or medicinal plant of importance which was not known to the Indian.[24]

Studying effigy pottery and ornaments is an excellent way to learn the type of dress, hair-dress and ornaments used by the early groups. It is almost impossible, however, to study their clothing, as most of them are depicted "sans robe," only paint and beads. One of our effigy figures represents a large female, painted bright red with dark stripes around her breasts and a chevron design on her arms. This figure was unusual in that she had a very handsome headdress or head covering, instead of the usual headdress found on female effigy pots.

Some of the most beautiful historic Indian robes in the world are to be seen at the Heye Foundation of the American Indian in New York City. Designers go there to study them for present-day fashions. One robe of ermine is especially beautiful. The wrappings of one female have always impressed me, for everything seemed to be of such soft material—a rabbit skin cape made of twisted strands of rabbit fur; a necklace of silk worm cocoons; the silky down of milk weed pods, and various other soft products.

Pottery effigy figures of the female are invariably plump, so I don't think the Mound Builder ladies bothered about diets and calories. Obesity evidently was a sign of beauty, as in some Oriental countries today.

When the new bridge was built across the Ohio River at Henderson, Kentucky, in excavating for the caissons a female effigy water bottle was taken out intact. This is probably not duplicated anywhere. The hair is combed straight back from the brow, fastened at the nape of the neck, and left hanging. Incised lines, equidistant, portray the teeth of the comb in the hair, and instead of the opening being in the back of the head, as is usual in effigy water bottles, the opening was made between the shoulders in the back. The figure is shown in a kneeling position, and both top and bottom of the ears are pierced, instead of the usual single lobe openings, as was the custom. It is one of my favorite effigies, and it has given me much information as to the profile and contour of the head.

From old DeBatz engravings we learn that some of the men shaved their heads and had a cockscomb effect, something like the historic Indian scalp lock. From our effigies we find that some parted their hair in the middle and had a chignon or twist at the back. Others had a bun of hair above each ear. Sometimes the hair was arranged on the head to look almost like a diadem or crown. Many of the effigy pots that I have excavated show this type of hair-dress. Several show the hair down the back. But it is not like the hanging braids of the historic Indian nor the queue of the Chinese, but more like the peruke that George Washington wore, as it was fastened at the base of the neck and left loose. The only likeness that I have seen similar to the Chinese queue is a perfect piece of pottery that was turned up by the plow at the Etowah-Tomlin site near Cartersville, Georgia. Fortunately it was unbroken. The figure has a hat on the head, similar to a farmer's straw hat. The unique part is that there is a hole in the top of the crown through which the braid of hair extends down the back as far as the hips. It is so perfectly modeled that the strands of the braid can be seen the entire length of the braid to the hole in the crown of the hat.

One of the most interesting effigies that I have ever excavated gave me a hearty laugh after I had washed it and the features were revealed. It was an artist's attempt to portray a one-eyed person, and it was excellently done by a native craftsman. One eye was made wide and staring and on the opposite side of the face there was no eye at all, only a blank space. The headdress was very well done and looked as if it had been copied from one made from split cane in the shape of a diadem.

Older men wore their hair in a knot above the forehead. Sometimes both sexes formed their hair in a long roll, like a horse tail, and bound it around the head with leather or beads. Long hair was a mark of distinction, and women's hair was cut off only for mourning or as a punishment for some crime. Their hair was black and coarse, and oil of nuts, sunflower seed, and animal fat were used to make it shine, as well as their body. During a period of war, hair was sometimes worn differently.

None of the Indians, prehistoric or historic, had beards. They used clam shells to pluck the hair, comparable to people using the lids of a gold watch to pull out hair. These shells were sharpened and used like tweezers. The same custom prevailed in Peru, as similarly sharpened clam shells were found in ancient burials. Copper tweezers have been found in Mexico.

On festive occasions, the Indian liked to wear a flower above the ear in the manner of a Spanish señorita. He also favored a stuffed bird, a tuft of feathers, or his enemy's dried hand. The hand was symbolical. We find many instances of its use on pottery and ornaments. On the outer wrapping of a mummy in Peru, I noticed the painted imprint of a hand. Perhaps it was made as a seal by some beloved relative. In some instances, on ruins in Europe one may see the imprint of a hand, perhaps the signature of the builder. Savages left the stains of a red hand across the mouth, indicating that they had drunk the blood of a foe. One of the most unusual pendants excavated here is made of shell in the shape of a hand with fingers extended, the design of a cross in dots, surrounded by two circles, on the palm. This pendant must have been very beautiful when first made, as it still shows the lovely iridescent colors of the shell.

The hand, in association with other symbols, is well illustrated in pottery, as shown from the Moundville, Alabama, tumuli. At Carthage, Alabama, a dark stone disc was found. Engraved on one side is an extended hand with fingernails. On the back of the hand is the familiar symbolical, all-seeing eye, and entwined around the hand and eye, near the edge of the disc, are two entwined rattlesnakes, with rattles in a conventionalized design of the plumed serpent. At the far edge of the disc are seventeen small notches—symbolical, no doubt. The reverse side is plain, with the exception of three incised circular lines around the edge of the disc.

It is an ordinary occurrence to find fabric in caves, for the atmospheric conditions tend to preserve the material, but it is unusual to find fabric in mounds. It. has to be preserved through metallic salts of copper or by carbonization.

Dr. Warren K. Morehead excavated some fabric with a colored design in the Etowah-Tomlin mounds, near Cartersville, Georgia, and some of the finest fabric ever uncovered was found in the Siep Mound in Ohio. Its preservation was due to having been placed between two copper breast plates.

In Mr. Eli Lilly's handsome publication, *Prehistoric Antiquities of Indiana,* he states, "Only one find of prehistoric fabric has thus far been made in Indiana." The piece of fabric was so small and finely woven that it was necessary to magnify it for study and photographing.

In Alabama, archæological research by the Tennessee Valley Authority has revealed a quantity of fabric, preserved by the oxidation of copper. Dr. Fay Cooper Cole informed me personally of this recent find but the scientific reports have not been published as yet.

I had always had a suppressed desire to find the actual fabric of the Mound Builder. This dream was realized on March 5, 1938, when an unusual fabric container was excavated from a portion of Mound D here at the King Mounds. Due to carbonization, the type of weave and material can be determined. The bag or container was filled with charred prehistoric corn and cobs. The corn was much larger than any we had found previously; apparently the largest ears had been placed in the bag for next year's planting, similar to the custom of the historic Cherokee Indian.

With both the prehistoric and historic Indian, many ceremonials accompanied the planting and harvesting of maize. According to the legend handed down to the Cherokees, seven ears of the current crop were put carefully aside in order to attract the maize god to the new crop, so it would have his blessing and grow and flourish. When the new corn was ripe a great ceremony took place, and only those who had fasted and purified themselves were permitted to take part. The seven ears of corn which had been saved from the previous year's harvest were then eaten. In the fall, at harvest time, seven ears were again put aside. In eating the first corn after the dance, care was observed not to blow upon the maize to cool it, for fear of causing a wind storm which might beat down the standing crop in the field.

The prehistoric Indian utilized from Mother Nature all the wonderful materials at hand to add to his comfort and pleasure. He didn't have to worry about shelter, heat, food, Easter bonnets, or any of the troubles of our present day.

CHAPTER VII

ORNAMENTS

Most primitive peoples loved ornaments. Some very exquisite specimens may be seen in the National Museum in Mexico City, said to have been found in the Monte Albán Tombs, Oaxaca, Mexico. Tomb number seven revealed the richest archæological finds ever made on the American continents, and prove that the ancient peoples of Oaxaca had attained high cultural advancement. The collection in the National Museum is very colorful with its jewels of amber, jet, silver and turquoise; gold necklaces set with rows and rows of pearls, coral and jade, with hanging gold ornaments containing little bells; high filigree headdresses, breast plates, bracelets, masques; exquisitely carved tiger bones and batons; and other innumerable things, all gorgeous.

A vase carved out of rock crystal is most beautiful; with a little imagination it could be a crystallized tear. The gold used is very yellow in shade, comparable to that used by old goldsmiths whose art one sees in collections in the Uffizi Gallery and Pitti Palace in Florence, Italy.

Señorita Amelia Martinez del Rio, who helped excavate the Monte Albán Tombs, presented me with a replica of one of the jewels that had been copied for her personal use. It is a filigree pendant and represents the universe. It was very interesting to see the few remaining rare Codices and hear her translate their meanings.

The Mound Builder also loved ornaments but he didn't have quantities of gold, silver, jade or coral like the Indians in Mexico. Instead, he used iron ore, or hematite, quartz, quartzite, rock crystal, and various other materials, and made plummets to hang around the neck. Beautiful ear-bobs or labrets for ear, nose, and lip were made out of pottery, bone, fluorspar, copper, shell and cannel coal.

Cannel coal was used to make pendants, rings, and gorgets. We have never found coal ash in any excavation. It is reported to have been found, however, in the Southwest. Cannel coal was either too precious to the Mound Builder in the Mississippi Valley or he didn't know that it would burn.

The headdresses of the Mound Builder were of various kinds, some being very elaborate. Feathers were used by both sexes as marks of distinction; also quills of large birds. Sometimes the horns of buffalo were worn on the head by the men, with the tail behind. Even in our times, especially in the Northern states, one sees fox or raccoon tails on automobiles, flying in the breeze. Stuffed bird heads were used as headdresses, and deer antlers, deer hoofs, and rattlers were prized.

Sometimes snake skins, stuffed with moss and tied by the tail, were used to hang down on the side of the head. A dead rat was a favorite ornament, and they were known to put a live snake in the lobe of the ear. That was a huge success and most entertaining when the snake would coil around the neck, and hiss in the face of the too inquisitve.

Some of the handsomest ornaments were made from mica. It was also used for mirrors. The nearest source for mica was the Carolinas and the Appalachian Mountains. Considering the limited means of navigation, that was a long distance for the Mound Builder, so it had to be brought in by inter-tribal relations or by trade and commerce. As a rule, mica is not found indiscriminately with other artifacts. It seems to be set apart. It was used not only for ornaments, but as offerings with the burials. One of our little infant burials is surrounded by pieces of mica, proving parental love, for it was probably the most precious thing they had to place in the burial.

On a trip through the Great Smokies not long ago, we stopped at one of the famous mica mines, a source undoubtedly of prehistoric mining. At the present time, however, it is being mined for an entirely different purpose than that used by the Mound Builder— the manufacture of electrical appliances, as it is a non-conductor of electricity. One of the owners of the mine reported that the mine was producing a net profit of five thousand dollars a week. That seems a rather extravagant figure, however.

Many, many beads were used by the early peoples. Any number of shells were available, so he might have as many as he wished to decorate his person. They were large, small, cushion-shaped, round, pointed, elongated, flat, disc-shaped, and spherical. Sometimes thirty yards of beads were fastened around the neck and arms, crossed over the breast and back, passing down between the legs to the feet and around the ankles. They were also used in headdresses, bracelets, earrings, pendants, and gorgets. Sashes were trimmed with them which could be thrown across the shoulders.

Beads were made out of animal teeth, stone, shell, bone, clay, seeds, wood, nuts, granite, jasper, sand-stone, greenstone, quartz, quartzite, catlinite, copper, slate, fluorspar, and other materials.

The Abnaki Indian's finery consisted only of beads, of shell or stone, some of which were made in various designs or figures, five or six inches in length, and used to plait the hair which he wore in a knot above the ears and back of the head. He also used ear pendants, collars, and garters. Sometimes beads and paint were the sum total of their clothing. They were so covered with paint oftentimes, that it looked like a dress or robe.

The female found in a mound burial at the Aztalan group of mounds in Wisconsin had three belts or long strings of shell beads. They could have been on a cape, but nothing was found except the beads.

The Mound Builder liked noise, and sometimes had

copper croisettes, shells, bracelets of pearl, gorgets and necklaces hanging from threads of deer sinew which he used as ornaments. It is said they soaked deer ribs in boiling water to make them soft and pliable; then they could be made into ornaments of any desired shape, and polished smooth like ivory. Hairpins were made out of bone and shell. Numerous times I have found these, criss-crossed at the top of the skull in a burial, indicating they were used as hair ornaments.

Some of the hairpins were made out of shell with a reverse spiral whirl; others had a knob on the top. This type was excavated also at the Etowah site in Alabama. The ones we find at the King Mounds are made from the hardest bone of the deer and other animals, are highly polished, and look like chop sticks.

Women had small slits in their ears, and men had large ones. They used pearls, sea shells, fish bladders blown up to resemble pearls, beast claws, legs of fowls, eagles, turkeys, hawks, and claws for ear ornaments. It was a terrible disgrace if the ears were slit accidentally, while preparing for the insertion of pendants. Sometimes women had strands of pearls in the ears hanging to the waist. The men wore five or six copper pendants in either lobe, bone carved into figures to represent birds and fish, and ornaments set with pearls and copper.

The use of shells as personal adornment may be traced back almost to primeval dawn, or to the time of Adam and Eve. In caves of France and Italy, along

with ivory, mammoth, and reindeer bones, shell necklaces and bracelets were discovered. In the Swiss Lake
Dweller excavations they have also been found.

Chroniclers of the De Soto expedition write that De
Soto found pearls the size of peas. In Ohio, during the
course of twenty years, a veritable king's ransom in
fresh-water pearls has been uncovered in the mounds.
Unfortunately corroded by the acid of the earth and
by having been used as burnt offerings, the commercial
value has been destroyed. But to the archæologist they
are precious, as they tell the story of adornment, personal effort, trade, commerce, and of lost beauty. I
have always hoped that we might find pearls in our
work, but the people whose remains we have uncovered
evidently did not wear beads, as we have found very
few, and it may have been taboo or not their custom to
wear them.

One of the greatest finds of recent years was made
at Spiro, Oklahoma. Unfortunately, the initial discovery was made by people who were interested in digging
and selling material rather than keeping the necessary
records that are so essential in archæological work.
Thousands and thousands of pearls, ornaments, masks,
beads, monolithic axes, copper, pottery of various
shapes and types, besides other valuable relics, were
found.

Wooden discs, covered with copper foil, were used
as ear ornaments. In one of our burials, two handsome
large earrings, carved from wood and covered with a

thin plating of beaten copper, were found near the head. These rings encircle seven-pointed stars and are beautifully preserved by the metallic salts caused by the oxidation of the copper. Wood has always played an important part in the life of man. It has been used for tools, implements, ornaments, and in defense.

Some very handsome gorgets were made out of shell. Engraved upon the shell were the cross, human figures, snakes, birds, spiders, and other animals. Some of the edges were beautifully scalloped with conventional designs of dots. An interesting one in the collection at the Smithsonian Institution (which was found at Eddyville, Kentucky), is a saucer-shaped gorget, five inches in diameter. It represents a discus or discoidal thrower. He had long bead necklaces around the neck and ornaments on the legs and arms. In his ear is a disc from which a long pendant ornament hung. He wore a short skirt, with pendants and gorgets hanging in the front, something like a Scotchman's purse. On his feet were moccasins.

Prehistoric peoples had great admiration for beauty and, being ingenious, utilized everything within their reach to create beautiful objects. Fortunately for archæology, two of the largest fluorspar deposits in the world are located in the Mississippi Valley, one at Rosiclare, Illinois, and the other at Marion, Kentucky. By being near these deposits, the prehistoric peoples learned of the great beauty in quality and color of this material, and mined, shaped, and carved it into handsome ornaments which we, of this generation, have been fortunate to find. Otherwise, prehistoric fluorspar ornaments would be unknown, as these veins of deposits are the only ones found in the Mississippi Valley.

The finest fluorspar ornaments known may be seen in the King collection at the King Mounds, better known as the Ancient Buried City, at Wickliffe, Kentucky. There are forty-seven pieces in the collection. One unusual piece is a small, squat effigy figure, carved out of pale pink fluorspar.

Notwithstanding that beads, ear-bobs, pendants and gorgets have been covered for centuries in graves, fire pits, and kitchen middens, and subjected to the elements, having been found buried near the surface, they still show beauty in color and design.

The pendants are unusually interesting; one exquisitely carved squirrel about an inch in length is a translucent amethyst in color and has a bushy tail curved over the back. This was discovered on the Cumberland River, near Eddyville, Kentucky. Also near Eddyville was found a pendant of a deep purple color, revealing an excellent attempt on the part of the artisan to depict a human face. The profile shows a long, well-accentuated nose, high cheek bones, and slit eyes, with the hair looped over the forehead—but no mouth. There is a hole in the top for suspension around the neck.

At the Kincaid Mounds on the Ohio River near

Unionville, Illinois, ten miles from Paducah, Kentucky, were found several fluorspar ornaments. One, a large figurine, grayish pink in color, has no fractures in it, the fluorspar being the same grade now utilized in laboratories for scientific lenses. A hole for suspension had been drilled through the entire figure. This is an exceptionally fine specimen because of the size, workmanship, and beauty of the crystal. The delicacy of the carving denotes a skilled artisan.

The above-mentioned fluorspar objects were found by three generations of the Kincaid family who entered the land from the Government. The University of Chicago has excavated this site for several seasons under the very capable direction of Dr. Fay Cooper Cole, Chairman of the Department of Anthropology at the University. In the course of the excavations, they have found a number of fluorspar ornaments.

Several lavender ear-bobs, a bead of white fluorspar, and a small yellow and pink pendant, shaped like a teardrop, were found at the King Mounds in Wickliffe, Kentucky, and at the Green Adams Mounds, near Hickman, Kentucky, a small yellow pear-shaped pendant was upturned by the plow.

In the King Mounds were also found two pendants, an unfinished round, white bead, and a polished, rectangular piece, shading from palest lavender to deep purple in color. One of the pendants is an excellently carved face, scarcely an inch in length, of translucent shades of amethyst. It has a hole for suspension. This

[80]

Male burial with copper ornaments

Part of the fluorspar collection of jewels excavated at the King Mounds—(1) Figurine of clear fluorspar; (2) Dark purple fluorspar figurine; (3) Delicately wrought workmanship in fluorspar excavated with bundle burial; (4) Fluorspar ornament used in the ear or lip; (5) Fluorspar object made to represent squirrel; (6) Fluorspar ornament; (7–8) Fluorspar labrets or lip plugs was found near the skull, the mandible inverted, in a bundle burial. Another piece is dark blue and pointed in shape.

In the Beckwith Collection at Cape Girardeau, Missouri, there is a beautifully wrought owl, while in the McPheeters family collection in Clinton, Kentucky, there is an almost exact duplicate in size, coloring and workmanship of the one uncovered with the bundle burial at Wickliffe.

In Mound D at the King Mounds, during the summer of 1935, a very unusual and large pendant of white fluorspar, rectangular in shape, with rounded corners showing evidences of having been surrounded by copper, was unearthed. Because of the fragility of this material, the artist showed great skill in his carving.

Carl, our colored man, excavated this pendant and brought it to me. It happened to be the day before Colonel King's birthday, so I held it as a surprise; he was delighted because it is one of the largest and finest specimens that have ever been excavated. By coincidence, during the past summer, at the same time as the previous discovery, Carl excavated another piece of fluorspar in the shape of a small bird, with wings outstretched. It is deep purple in color. This was found in Mound F.

These artifacts all represent infinite care and patience, as well as great skill and love for beauty, on the part of the prehistoric peoples.

Teeth of beaver, wolf and other animals were used. One necklace that we uncovered in an excavation several years ago consists of alternate perforated wolf and bear teeth, with a round pottery bead between each tooth. The teeth were perforated by drilling a small hole in the root. Often the holes were bored from each side to meet in the center; others were bored in one operation, completely through the tooth.

In one excavation, large bear incisors were found with two holes bored in them at an angle in such a manner that the holes did not extend through the teeth. This was so they could be strung or sewed on fabric and skins without showing any portion of the thread or holes.

Mexicans called obsidian the "Shining God" and held it in high esteem. Caused by volcanic action, it is everywhere in the fields in Mexico, like rocks in New England and Kentucky. We picked up innumerable pieces also in the fields around Teotihuacan. It was used for many purposes. The sacrificial knife was made from it, and mirrors were fashioned out of solid obsidian. Beautiful obsidian artifacts have been found in mounds in Ohio, Oregon, and other Western States. Obsidian is obtained also from the Rocky Mountain region.

In the Museum at Mexico City I was attracted by the teeth in an exhibit. On one of the front teeth was a black dot. In examining it more closely, I saw the enamel had been removed and the tooth set with obsidian! Turquoise was also used as an ornament in the teeth. In this country it is said diamonds have been set in the teeth for ornaments, but I have never seen them.

On the expedition of Tulane University, New Orleans, Louisiana, to the Uloa Valley in Honduras, a skull was found on a river bank. After it had been washed, the teeth revealed incisors that had been filed according to the custom, and three of the upper front teeth had been inlaid with turquoise. The most unusual thing about this skull was the jade bead imbedded in the palate on the right side behind the front teeth. Possibly this was that man's money for the journey into the new world. Many times I have excavated numbers of quartz pebbles in burials. They were either used in rattles, the skin having long since gone to dust, or in gourds for ceremonials, or in sling shots such as David of Biblical fame used to slay the giant. Possibly they represented money for the next world. Some day we shall know, as each year we learn more about the customs of prehistoric man.

CHAPTER VIII

FOOD

INVARIABLY people think that ours is the only age that has had food in quantity and variety. We think we have so much food of every kind, but the Mound Builder also had quantities of food and from the great number of animal, fish, and fowl bones found, he evidently dined abundantly and well. A doctor was here at the King Mounds one day and was surprised at the great quantities of fish, fowl, and animal bones. "Why!" he said, "they had plenty of Vitamin D."

In Mound D, of the King Mounds, is concrete evidence of prehistoric dining. In one of the house sites is a concave fire pit, two feet in diameter, which shows evidence of great heat, as it has a layer of fire-hardened clay, baked almost to a brick. Around this fire-pit are three holes which must have held three posts as a tripod to hang cooking vessels over the fire; and deer, bear, or whatever meat they were cooking could likewise be suspended. Near the fire pit are the remains of a feast, a charred heap of chinkapin nuts, hickory nuts, walnuts, pecans, beech nuts, pig nuts, maize kernels, beans similar to lima beans, squash seed, bones of turkey, squirrel, bear, deer, beaver, wolf, opossum, raccoon, and other species of animal, fowl and fish, all bearing definite proof of prehistoric dining. The women ground the maize. A large flat rock was placed between the feet and legs, and another small cylindrical one held in the hand.

Mortar and pestles, which were used to grind nuts and to pound the meat, played an important part in the Mound Builder's domestic life. Many countries followed a similar custom. Chile had wood and stone mortars; Costa Rica used lava rock and stone for metates. In Haiti, an unusual heart-shaped stone mortar was excavated. Some of the pestles are highly polished on the ends from grinding and pounding, and many of them look like our modern rolling pins. There is this exception, however, that if the prehistoric wife had become angry and hit her good husband over the head, he soon would have gone to the Happy Hunting Grounds, as they were made of stone and were quite heavy.

Many animal bones, particularly those of the deer, are found split. These were split by the early inhabitants in a way similar to those found in ancient caves of Europe. People liked to eat the marrow then just as we do today.

The maize of the Mound Builder had been domesticated from the Mexican Teocentli plant, and from this they made hoe cake or bread of some kind. All the wild fruits and vegetables were used, so they had a balanced diet.

Women have always been interested in food and

bargains. We know the prehistoric inhabitants believed in barter and trade and no doubt the women had their share in the bargaining, just as we women today love sales or dollar day! What woman can withstand a bargain? It is instinctive in us, perhaps a hold-over or heritage from the barter and trade of the aboriginal peoples.

Animals and birds have been part of the family, so to speak, from the beginning of time. The story of the animals marching two by two into Noah's Ark in Biblical days is known to all of us. There is a charming ancient legend about the humming bird and tobacco. Tobacco was used in ceremonials and regarded as sacred incense. It was sprinkled in the fire during illness and when smoked or chewed it was called "fire to hold in the mouth." It was also used as food, as illustrated in the following story.

According to this old legend, in the beginning of the world, when people and animals were all the same, there was only one plant to which everyone had to come for tobacco. Some geese stole this and carried it far away to the south. People were suffering without it, and one old woman grew so thin and weak everyone said she would die soon unless she could get tobacco to keep her alive.

Different animals offered to go, one after another, the larger ones and then the smaller ones, but the Dogulku geese saw and killed each animal before it could get to the plant. The little mole tried to reach it, but the geese saw his track and killed him when he came out. At last the humming bird offered but everyone said he was entirely too small, and he might as well stay at home. He begged them to let him try, so they showed him a plant in a field and told him how he should get it. The next moment he was gone, and they saw him sitting on the plant. In a moment he was back again but no one had seen him coming or going, because he was so swift. "That is the way I'll do," said the humming bird, so they let him try.

He flew off to the south, and when he came in sight of the tobacco, the geese were watching all about it. They could not see him, however, for he was so small and flew so swiftly. He darted down on the plant and snatched off the top with the leaves and seeds, and was off again before the geese knew what had happened. Before he got home, the old woman had fainted and they thought she was dead, but he blew the smoke into her nostrils and with a cry of "Tobacco!" she opened her eyes and was alive again.

I was interested in reading in the excellent book by Mabel Cook Cole and Fay Cooper Cole, entitled *The Story of Man; His Earliest Appearance and Development to the Portals of History,* an account of snail eaters of Africa. The only food I couldn't manage in Brittany was snails. They are a great delicacy to the Breton people and my *bonne's* eyes would shine when she put large, black-headed pins at our plates. That meant a course of snails! They are served alive in the shell and one is supposed to pierce them with the pin and draw them out of the shell and eat them! They wiggled too much for me, and to the Breton people's amazement I declined that course whenever it was served.

At first, *les crevettes* were a little difficult for me, but eventually I could pull off the whiskers and crunch them down with the best of them. *Les crevettes* are a little like our grasshoppers in shape. It was always a surprise to me that my small son would eat cuttle fish and refuse every other kind, for cuttle fish, although they look well in bird-cages, have a very racy, strong taste, according to my palate.

We have excavated deer, elk, antelope, raccoon, squirrel, catamount, panther, wolf and fox bones; also wild turkey, geese, swans, ducks, cranes, quails, eagles, hawks, owls, and many species of fish, particularly the mussel shells and terrapin.

Mussel shells were used to make beads and some of the finest ornaments of the Mound Builders. They are not affected by the acids of the earth, and when found, notwithstanding they may have been in the ground for centuries and are very soft, the exquisite, iridescent colors of mother of pearl are still beautiful. Not long ago, I noticed that it is quite fashionable to serve caviar in mother-of-pearl dishes, so we are imitating the prehistoric peoples.

Spoons were made from mussel shells, some of which are very handsome. Most of them seem to have been

Woven cane basket and prehistoric corn or maize and cobs

made for use in the right hand, as only a few are for the left hand. Spoons could have been made out of wolf-ears, according to a legend. We find so many terrapin shells that the Mound Builder undoubtedly knew this story.

One day the opossum and the terrapin went out hunting to find ripe persimmons. They found a tree filled with delicious ripe fruit. The opossum climbed the tree and threw the persimmons down to the terrapin. Before he could get them, a wolf darted in and ate every one of them. So the opossum threw down a bone which choked and killed the wolf, whereupon the terrapin decided the wolf's ears would make very useful spoons, and so he cut them off!

As it was the custom to set a jar of gruel outside the door, the terrapin stopped at various houses and sampled the gruel with his new spoons. The wolves held a meeting and decided to boil the terrapin in a pot, for he had killed a wolf and was using his ears for spoons. The terrapin laughed and said he would kick the pot to pieces. Then they determined to burn him in a hot fire, but he said he would put out the fire. Then they decided to throw him in the deepest hole in the river and drown him. He cried and begged them not to do that, but they paid no attention and threw him in. SPLASH! That was just what he was waiting for and he dived under the water and came up on the other side and got away. Some say he hit against a rock when he struck the river, which broke his back into a dozen

pieces. The legend states further that he sang a medicine song, "I have sewed myself together, I have sewed
myself together!" and the pieces came together. But
the scars remain on his shell to this day.

Many caves yield finds of the aboriginal peoples.
The old extinguished hearths of French caves show
man's early acquaintance with the products of the
chase and spoils of the sea. Food was prepared by heat-
ing stones and throwing them into the water or soup.
Most of the pottery vessels could not stand too much
heat. Hot coals and ashes also were used to cook the
food. Pointed sticks and slivers of cane held the fresh
meats above the flame, as we roast our meats over the
picnic fires.

It was a custom with the prehistoric peoples to pro-
vide food for the journey into the Unknown and with
most burials we find evidence of these provisions.
Loaves of bread, made without yeast, have been found
in Neolithic pile villages in Switzerland. Milling
stones were associated with female burials, indicating
that their use was woman's work. Peas, lentils, wheat,
barley, seeds of wild cherry, plum, apple, grapes, and
bones of fish were found at various levels, invaluable
data for research.

"The dog, hog, ox, sheep, and goat were all found in
the lowest archæological level at Auvernier pile village
on Lake Neuchâtel. Milk and its products were made
use of in Neolithic times. The remains of at least seventy species of animal occur in Neolithic lake dwell-

ings; some of these were domesticated, others were not." [25]

In this part of the Americas, the early migrants on the Pacific Coast had nuts of the acorn trees and different species of fish. In the Rocky Mountain district, there were small game, seeds and roots before agriculture was developed. On the Great Plains roamed immense herds of buffalo which could be driven over the cliffs and killed. However, until the Indian obtained the horse he found buffalo hunting both difficult and dangerous, in spite of his knowledge of the bow. North of the Plains the caribou ranged and bands of men who lived off the herds were forced to move constantly to follow the game. Along the Arctic Seas were the Eskimos who lived primarily on marine animals.[26]

Before agriculture was developed the people in the lake and river districts lived on game, wild products and maple sugar. In the principal diet of the aboriginal group of the Mound Builder here in Kentucky, maize, deer, wild turkey, duck, and fish predominate.

Food, shelter, and clothing have always been man's prime needs. They are profoundly influenced by climate and geographic conditions.

CHAPTER IX

POTTERY AND CULTURAL
INDICATIONS

ARCHÆOLOGISTS agree that pottery undoubtedly is the most valuable single index in determining cultures that we have, as it was more universally used than any other item and entered into the daily life. It is fortunate for us and posterity that fragments of pottery or potsherds are imperishable; otherwise most of the story of the prehistoric pottery and weaving would be lost for all time. The prehistoric examples of textiles are rare because of the perishability of the material. In our modern, stream-lined world, glass has now been perfected so that fabric is woven from it which is practically nondestructible by fire. I wonder if it won't be as perishable as the Mound Builder's fabric after the interim of centuries.

There was no potter's wheel on this hemisphere prior to the arrival of the Europeans. All pottery was made by hand. Often the soft clay was formed into shape and placed in a basket to dry, and thus the impression of the weave of the basket was left on the pot; otherwise the vessel was formed into the desired shape and wrapped in a piece of cloth or fabric and placed in the sun to dry. The design or weave of the cloth left indentures in the soft clay and a lasting record of their weaving and textiles. This is designated as the negative design of the weave.

In order to secure the positive or actual outline, soft clay or plaster can be applied to the surface and the actual reproduction of the fabric which perished centuries ago may be obtained. After the pottery was sundried, it was fired in open fires or placed in an enclosed kiln, as is indicated by the irregularly burned surfaces of the vessel. We have uncovered quite a number of pottery balls, probably used in games or in the firing of pottery to keep the vessels apart.

Usually people visualize the pottery of the Mound Builder as poorly-fired terra cotta. On the contrary, many of the pottery items are beautifully polished by hand, with a mixture of animal fat and pigments. For mineral dyes, black was secured by using carbon in some form. Charcoal, soot, coal and graphite served this purpose. Ocher supplied shades of yellow, red, brown and white. Slate was used for gray. Iron oxide and iron tri-oxide, or paint rocks, also furnished many of the colors, such as brown, yellow, and red. Plants, roots and herbs were collected, prepared, and made into vegetable dyes.

Pottery is found particularly in refuse piles or kitchen midden in mounds, village sites, the hearth or fire pits, ashes and burials. Coiled pottery represents one of the first methods known in the technique of the construction of pottery. Rolls of clay were coiled to any desired shape. The prehistoric potter used plain, incised, engraved, appliqué, roughened, combed, stamped, punched or punctate, cord and fabric impressions; also scrolls, spirals, trailed and modifications of the circle in designs. Two methods were employed in marking and designing pottery—one while the pottery was soft and before it was air-dried or burned in a kiln; the second method is to incise or scratch after the drying and burning. The markings which are made in the soft surfaces are much deeper and broader. A common form of pottery, made by the North American Indian, is that of the gourd, with ears or holes perforated at the rim for suspending the vessel over the fire.

Incised patterns on the surfaces bear a curious resemblance to the simple linear devices seen on ancient sepulchral pottery of other countries. Some of the savage art shows great exaggeration and the carvings exhibit most extraordinary characters. However, these potters had great imitative skill and ability in modeling clay.

The principal finds of Clarence B. Moore at Moundville, Alabama, on the Warrior River, were pottery. Many of the pieces may be seen at the George T. Heye Museum of the American Indian in New York City. Other interesting artifacts from the Moundville site are on display at Tuscaloosa, at the museum on the beautiful university campus. Colonel King has been director of the Museum for many years and I had the honor of being honorary curator of archæology of that institution.

Through the efforts of Dr. Carl Guthe, head of the Department of Anthropology at the University of Michigan, Ann Arbor, a ceramic repository has been created there for study and research. Material from many states in the Mississippi Valley is now revealing an interesting story of similarity and difference. Under the capable direction of Dr. James B. Griffin of the ceramic repository, much detailed work has been done. He states that through his efforts in the study of sherds in the Norris Dam territory he has been able to make a report which fills the gap in the archæological history of the Southeast.[27]

Where the Little and St. Francis Rivers have their confluence near Marked Tree, Arkansas, more painted ware of a certain type has been found than in any other site in the Mississippi Valley. Painted terra cotta ware with a heavy paint slip or covering reached a high state of development in this territory. Many of the zoomorphic forms are painted in solid red of deep hue, while others are painted in red and white designs. A large shallow bowl in an orange-red shade has the representation of a bear's head on one side, with well-defined nostrils, incisor teeth, eyes and ears, while another, painted red and white, depicts a turtle effigy with the small head extended from the shell resting on four feet. Still another is shaped like a goose with a long neck and an opening at the top in place of a head. It has four feet however.

There is a great variety of form, size, and decoration in the pottery at this particular site. To one familiar with the influence of various cultures, such as Adena, Fort, Ancient, Hopewell, Woodland and the Middle Mississippi cultures, it is easy to identify their individual characteristics. Aside from the fact that this is a type site, the predominant cultural indication is that of the middle Mississippi. The favorite color seems to be solid black with a highly finished gloss, made by vigorous polishing and rubbing.

The pottery complex is crushed or beaten mussel shell used as a tempering agent, and in rare cases a very small amount of grit tempered is found. Only a few cord markings made by a twine-covered potter's paddle have been excavated here, but further north, at the Kincaid mound on the Ohio River in Illinois, the principal fabric design was produced by the paddle. Twenty miles south of this site, on the Mississippi River in Kentucky, the same type of ware occurs in great quantities. The cord impressions found at Wickliffe, however, were produced by fabric wrappings rather than by a paddle or other mechanical devices. Fabric weaves have a great diversification as to spacing, ranging from the coarsest to the very finest weave, comparable to cotton cloth which is manufactured today.

Many of the pots are shallow, with single or double lugs, incised inside and out. Ornamentation was made

(1) Bear head made of pottery; (2) Owl head made of pottery—hole in top for suspension; (3) Owl head made of pottery. All excavated at the King Site

Flint cane knives used to split cane, one edge, longitudinal, polished from use. Excavated at the King Mounds

Painted turtle made of pottery. In the King Collection

Juice press types—small opening at bottom, large aperture top

Juice press types

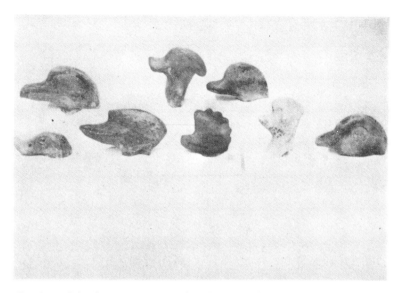

Duck and fowl types pottery heads, one with top knot, excavated from the King Mounds

Top—(1)Pottery head made to represent a fox; (2) quail; (3) dog.
Bottom—(1) deer; (2) raccoon; (3) bear or lizard
All excavated at King Mounds

by using a sharpened tool of bone to scratch or incise the ware. Others have designs made with the thumb nail. Those with handles or lugs remind me of old silver porringers and the silver wine tasters of Richelieu's time in France. They are also somewhat similar in shape to the Quimper bowls of Brittany.

I have always hoped that a burial urn might be uncovered at Wickliffe, but as yet none has been excavated. Burial urns have been found, however, in Tennessee, Alabama, Missouri, Louisiana, Mississippi, and other states. In Brazil and Colombia, large painted pottery urns with effigy heads have been excavated.

In one of the mounds of the Scioto Valley in Ohio, a large bowl was found inverted over a skull, used partially, no doubt, as a burial urn. In another mound in Ohio, a curiously ornamented urn, having a capacity of six quarts, was found. It had a cover which fitted down over the vessel for six inches. One interesting, large, shallow bowl or plate in our collection contained only the right and left forearms of an adult, which had apparently been severed at the elbows. These had been carefully crossed at the wrist and placed in the bowl.

We have recovered an entirely new type of vessel for the Mississippi Valley. In shape, taking into consideration all factors, a better name for it is a juice press. There is a large wide opening at the top and a small hole at the bottom. The size and shape would indicate such a use, as a small piece of fabric inside would have served the purpose of retaining any seeds or coarse vegetable matter inside the container and permit the extract to be collected in another vessel, as pressure was exerted from the top towards the small aperture in the bottom. The near-by hills, valleys, and bottom land furnish juice-bearing fruits and berries in great abundance; therefore, the one and only deduction is that the juice press was an independent invention and used for this purpose. It is possible that the juices were allowed to ferment and were used as wine or liquor. Most all groups have had liquid stimulants. Someone has suggested that since Kentucky has always been known for its liquor, the aboriginal peoples ran true to form.

Pottery, like the juice presses found here at the King Mounds, is characteristic of a definite culture. These are generally given the name of a typical station or type site where the material first is found and identified.

In Rössen, near Merseberg in Germany, handsome prehistoric pottery belonging to the Neolithic period has been excavated. This is known as the Rössen type. In Central Europe there are the Aunjetiz and Lausitz cultures. Pottery urn burials found in Germany, Poland, Bohemia, Moravia, and Austria represent these cultures. The iron age culture, according to Dr. George MacGurdy, is represented in eastern Germany and Poland by face urns very similar to the effigy pottery of the Mound Builder and clearly showing that man's activity all over the world has been somewhat similar in a general way.

Recently we secured two interesting face bowls or urns, one of which was excavated by Opie Reid in a ridge mound on the Hayes Keyes farm on the east bank of Little River, near State Road 40, half way between Marked Tree and Lepanto, Arkansas. The other was found near by. One of the bowls in the original was painted red inside and out, with the exception of the face, which was a lighter shade, made to represent the complexion, no doubt. It had holes in the rim for suspension, and six holes as ornaments in the ears. It is possible there may have been earrings through the holes when first made, comparable to the face urns found in Germany in which earrings or coils were found. The plain bowl is rather crudely made with holes in the ears but none for suspension. The hairdress was a coil around the forehead, ending in a chevron or leaf design, four inches in length and three inches in width at the end of the coil. With each bowl were two very fine shell masks, with perforations for the eyes and mouth. It has been suggested that they were masks used over faces of the dead, as Oriental nations use metal masks of the human face. An unusual pottery rattle, shaped like an egg, four inches in length and eight inches in circumference, with two holes at each end for suspension, was also found. Many of the human and zoomorphic effigy heads and handles that we excavate contain clay pellets which rattle when shaken.

Through the kindness of Mr. F. R. King, President of the Tennessee Valley Historical Society, we secured a large stone bowl, thirteen inches in height, with a flared top forty-two inches in circumference. It is ornamented with a large zig-zag pattern or design. A farmer on the Tennessee River in Gunterville, Alabama, overturned it with the plow one spring, and the next season uncovered a handsome ceremonial tobacco burner, weighing twenty-two pounds. This is a composite piece representing the head of a bear and the tail of a bird. On the top and middle of the body there is a large round opening, the body being encircled by a snake. No doubt both pieces were used in conjunction in ceremonials, as both the prehistoric and the historic Indian believed in the potency of tobacco.

In Wisconsin, the Lake Courte Oreilles band of Chippewa Indians had a Manitou or spirit rock, known as the pipe of the Manitou. The moccasined feet of the Indians had worn a deep trail to the rock where, according to the Indian tradition, if each Indian deposited a generous pinch of tobacco in the hollow on top of the stone the great spirit would appear and smoke his pipe and grant petitions or prayers in time of war and great trouble. Another medicine stone for tobacco offerings was located in the Northwest part of the Lac du Flambeau region.[28]

Many pottery trowels are found in the King Mounds. I was surprised to find them with infant skeletal material burials. Heretofore, many other things such as beads, tiny pots, effigy birds, and those representing the sun perch fish have been recovered; but the past few months have yielded pottery trowels for the first time with infant burials.

An unusual pottery trowel was excavated with an adult burial which has five holes for the fingers so that the trowel may be grasped very easily, as the fingers of the hand fit nicely in the holes. In Mexico, pottery trowels were shaped like an old-fashioned flat iron or mason's trowel. These were used in working adobe. Another tool expressing individuality is a chipped flint celt made with a definite hand grip for a handle instead of the usual blunt and clumsy type. Many large cooking pots and plates have been uncovered in the various excavations. Some of the effigy heads are unique and are an invaluable way to study hairdress and hair ornaments. An interesting stone pendant depicts a drawing of a wild goose flying on one side, and on the other is a stag with a flint in its side. Flaring lips on shallow bowls and erect animal effigies are very common.

From the unusual material excavated at the King Mounds, it is known as a type site for the middle Mississippi Valley territory. This is determined by the juice press, the sweat-houses, cane knives with the sharpened longitudinal edge for splitting cane, fluorspar industry, and sun and fire worship as indicated by orientation and the use of charcoal under the burials, and premeditated burnings of two temple buildings and a number of dwellings or house sites. Sun and fire worship has been more definitely established here than at any other site in the Mound Building area.

This locality was the center of the fluorspar industry. As Amsterdam is now the center for polishing diamonds, this site served as the center for polishing and perfecting fluorspar jewels. The mines were only a short distance away, and the raw material was secured by water transport or over land. In the course of our excavations, a complete cross-section is illustrated by the numerous finds, from the raw material in the different stages of workmanship to the finished product. A total of fifty pieces comprise this material, from the very plain to the most delicately wrought human faces, figurines, pendants and other jewelry.

In the King collection of over ten thousand carefully selected artifacts are some of the finest prehistoric effigy pottery, owls, pipes, bannerstones, ceremonials, flints and jewelry to be found in this country. This does not include fifty thousand or more spear and arrow points. In this collection of artifacts are effigy bowls representing fish, frogs, ducks, owls, bears, opossums and other animals. Many of the serpent effigies are very fine; one in particular has well-defined teeth, nose and eyes, with the tail wrapped around the neck of a smaller animal, similar to the plumed or feathered serpent design found in Mexico.

We have excavated three types of shallow plate, many of them measuring fourteen inches in diameter at least. Two types are similar, with the exception, however, that one has fabric impressions on the outside, showing that a fabric bag was used as a mold until it was air dried. The other type of the same size has no decoration and was not placed in a bag to dry. The third type of shallow plate is much smaller in size and made of a finer polished ware. It is decorated inside by an incised or scratched leaf motif and different variations of the triangle.

Some of the pottery effigy types are human caricatures, and the one representing a crouching woman, arms on knees, is seen so often that one is led to believe that she represents some malevolent goddess whose anger had to be averted in every household.

The sun and serpent must have been symbols in their mythology or a motif used in their art. It was used extensively as a design on their artifacts. One unusual ceremonial here of hematite represents a human face surrounded by a serpent on the outer edge with its tail in its mouth. The ceremonial is four inches in length, two and one-half inches in width and is an elongated circle in shape. This had some special significance in their religion, no doubt, as the serpent has been one of the predominant symbols among primitive nations. It prevailed in Egypt, Greece, Assyria, and Central America, and entered into the superstitions of the Celts, Hindoos, Chinese, and Mexicans. The ancient Celts erected structures in the form of serpents; the

Zuñi and Shawnee of the historic Indian used it as a totem. People have worshiped the sun through all the ages.

Returning recently from a journey, I was impressed anew with the great expanse of sky to be seen from the Temple Mound, which overlooks the confluence of the Mississippi and Ohio Rivers. It gives one a feeling of standing on the threshold of another world. I was enthralled at the marvelous colors of the setting sun; the centuries seemed to fold back and I visualized myself standing where the Mound Builder must have also stood and worshiped the sun.

In Egypt worship of the sun's rays is supposed to be the source which gives energy and life. At the Hotel Jungfraublich in Switzerland, dinner is never served until the sun sets over the majestic Jungfrau. At Easter time in California a great sunrise service is held out of doors. So in a way we are sun worshipers even today. There is an old proverb, "May your happiness last as long as the rays of the sun shine upon the earth."

CHAPTER X

FETISHES

It is surprising how many pet superstitions people have. Some of us have fewer than others, but I believe that, in spite of denials, everyone has his pet superstition. "A little learning is a dangerous thing," it is said. Until I read that to see a crow flying East was bad luck, I thought nothing of it; now, unconsciously, after seeing one crow flying East, I crane my neck in all directions, trying to find the second that will insure good luck. A famous editor in England always had his butler lead him blind-folded out of doors at the time of the new moon so he would not see it through glass but over his right shoulder. Other pet superstitions are to put the right shoe on first in the morning, never to walk under ladders, and to break a mirror—horrors! That meant seven years of bad luck. One time I broke a hand mirror and a series of misadventures took place inadvertently, so I suggested we take a ride to the country and throw away the mirror. When we arrived at the chosen spot I got out with the mirror, and as I stepped over a little ditch near a fence I was stung by a bee! Coincidence, no doubt, but naturally I blamed it on the mirror.

The negroes in the South have many superstitions.

Never, never, step over a broom; either pick it up or walk around it. (Walking around suits most of them better.) Never put a hat or umbrella on the bed and, heavens! never come in one door and go out another. And as for knocking on one's door, our colored house man said, "Oh! no, no, Ma'am, I knows I nevah would knock on my own do'." If you have warts, you must hide the dish rag. If you have a sty, rub the eye with a gold ring and say, "Sty, sty, go off my eye, go on the first passerby." A rabbit's foot is considered very lucky, and some people believe that before turning around one should make a cross on the ground with the foot. Did you know that the city of Los Angeles has a twelfth, a fourteenth, but no thirteenth street? This is also true in some city hotels, where there are no thirteenth floors. Some people think to find a four-leaf clover is good luck. A poem reads, "God put another one in just for luck; if you search, you will find where they grow."

Nearly everyone has some peculiarity or is superstitious to some degree. My olfactory powers are very highly developed and I am hyper-sensitive to odors. There are so many delightful smells—a kitchen on baking day, newly washed clothes dried in the sun, freshly bathed babies, harness shops, outdoors after a rain, ocean spray, a flower garden at night. I love perfume and consider it lucky. Possibly that is superstitious, but I feel happier whenever I use it.

When I was a very little girl I used to love to go to

the neighbor's house next door. She had a corner cupboard filled with beautiful old dishes that I admired immensely. She also had a perfumed soap that I adored. One day she came into the room where I was busily rubbing the perfumed soap over the dishes in the cupboard and asked, "What are you doing, honey?" I replied, "I am mafuming your dishes, Auntie Sote." In her kitchen was a cook stove that had a hearth on which was a bas relief of a train. Each day when she gave me a glass of milk and some of her delicious homemade thin ginger cookies, I insisted on sitting on the floor, eating them on the hearth, so that I could be on the train. The wanderlust attacked me early, reminding me of Edna St. Vincent Millay's line, "There isn't a train I wouldn't take, no matter where it's going." [29]

Aunt Sote was an insatiable reader. When I was seven years old she gave me a copy of Lamb's *Tales of Shakespeare*. It so influenced me that I named my two kittens Romeo and Juliet, but they both turned out to be Romeos. She was a brilliant woman, was conversant on all the problems of the day, and was an excellent business woman. She admired Henry James and used to remark that she was his contemporary. She was quiet and reserved but a woman of action. Her father married her to her cousin when she was very young and like the man at the funeral of his wife who said, "I never did like that woman," she never particularly cared for her husband. He had been unfaithful to her for years, so one day when he was away she had all his belongings packed and moved across the street. When he returned she told him he didn't live there any more. In later years, when our paths divided, her letters were a joy. Shortly before she passed on, she sent me one of her most prized possessions, an old gold quill pen, with a mother-of-pearl handle. She considered the pen very lucky, so the gift carried with it not only her love but some of her superstitions as well, for she was undoubtedly one of the most superstitious people who ever lived.

We have several black cats here at the King Mounds. Being a K.A.T. (Kappa Alpha Theta), I think they are very lucky. Two incidents in connection with the cats happened not long ago. A man saw one of them, gave it a quick look and said to his wife, "Oh! we'll never get home." I was also amused at the wife of another couple. When she saw one of the cats, she said, "Don't let that black cat cross my path. One crossed it the day I got married." Needless to say, the husband's face bore a peculiar expression.

In the course of the first excavations here, a large circus tent was placed over the Burial Mound. When the weather was cold one of the negroes preferred to sleep in the big tent near the skeletons that had been uncovered, so that he could have a large wood fire. This was in utter contrast to another negro who shined our shoes in the village. We often asked him when he was coming to see the excavations, and with the whites of his eyes predominating in his shiny black face, he answered, "No suh! Not me! I don't want to see any skiletens or hants."

One day while riding in the country, I noticed a little house whose back door was within a few feet of a cemetery. I mused aloud, "I shouldn't want to live near a cemetery like that"—and my husband replied, "Oh, no! You live right on top of one." That is not quite true, however, for no one knows what is in any ground until it is excavated.

The prehistoric peoples had their charms, amulets, and fetishes, just as the people of today have their lucky pieces.

Excavating determinedly one day, I came upon some small, hard objects. Before the dirt was taken away, I thought possibly they were beads, but upon completing the excavation I found they were concretions, supposed to be very lucky as the genitals of some ancient being. Concretions were held in high regard by certain groups and were evidence of phallic worship. If a young man carried them, they were believed to have been a valuable adjunct in his conquest with the ladies. In other words, they made him a real tarzan or he-man and it was not necessary to have had monkey glands injected. If a woman carried them, they were supposed to insure her having male children. Personally, I should think they would have been a bit heavy to carry around in one's pocket book or wear around the neck. Some of the types we find are quite indelicate. However, phallic worship prevailed with many prehistoric races.

Burning tobacco in time of trouble was an Indian superstition. The Indian also believed that wearing a bone or hair of a deceased relative would exercise a sort of guardianship. Hair wreaths and brooches are to be seen even today—a custom, no doubt, that has been carried down for countless ages. In Guiana, some tribes have their bones cleaned after death and distributed to the relatives. The Indian believed in wearing fetishes. Few hunters would think of venturing forth without one. They were thought to bring success, not only in the chase, but in other matters as well.

According to tradition, animal and bird fetishes were actual petrifications of the animals they represented and it was believed that the heart still lived, even though the body was changed to stone.

The Mountain Lion took precedent over all. He was Hunter God of the North. The Black Bear was supposed to be guardian and master of the West; the Badger was guardian of the South; the White Wolf of the East, and the Eagle was master of the upper regions. The Mole had complete mastership of the lower regions. These animals were supposed to have complete domination, and powers emanated from them. An illustration of the power of the Black Bear is shown in the Zuñi story of "Mi-tsi."

Mi-tsi was long a faithful member of the Little Fire order (Ma-ke-tsa-na-kwe), but he grew careless, neglected his sacrifices, and resigned his rank as "keeper of the medicines," from sheer laziness. In vain his fathers warned him but he only grew hot with anger. One day Mi-tsi went up on the mesas to cut corral posts. As he sat down to eat his dinner, a great black bear walked out of the thicket near at hand and leisurely approached him. Mi-tsi began to have sad thoughts of the warnings of his fathers. "Alas," he cried, "pity me, my father from the West-land!" In vain he promised to be a good Ma-ke-tsa-na-kwe. Had not Po-shai-an-k'ia commanded?

But the Black Bear seized him by the foot and pulled until Mi-tsi screamed from pain; but, cling as he would to the tree, the bear pulled him to the ground. Then he lay down on Mi-tsi and pressed the wind out of him until he fainted from the pain. Black Bear started to go, but eyed Mi-tsi. Mi-tsi kicked. Black Bear came and pressed his wind out again. It hurt Mi-tsi, and he said to himself, "Oh dear me! What shall I do? The father thinks I am not punished enough." So he kept very still. Then Black Bear went slowly away, looking at Mi-tsi all the while, until he passed a little knoll. Mi-tsi then crawled away and hid under a log. When he thought himself man enough, he started for Zuñi. He was sick for a long time, for Black Bear had eaten his foot. He still lives and limps, but he is a good Ma-ke-tsa-na-kwe. Who shall say that Po-shai-an-k'ia did not command?

From old legends we learn that shepherds often carried a fetish made out of beautiful fluorspar, carved to represent a large sheep, which was a protection against disease. It was good fortune when fetishes were found. They were prey gods of the medicine man. The mountain lion, white bear, knife-feathered monsters—hundreds of folklore tales have been written about them.

The mountain lion and coyote fetishes are the more plentiful, as a greater number of them was made originally, because of the power of the mountain lion and coyote. The mole fetish is very rare, because few were made of the mole, as he was less powerful.

Fetishes were held in possession of the shamans, and greatly venerated by them as mediators between themselves and the animals they represented. We have a bird and squirrel effigy made out of fluorspar which were, no doubt, used as fetishes. We find the bear and other animal fetishes. An unusual one is a bird, made out of pink chalcedony. Between its carved wings a small bird point was attached with a band of sinew wrapped around the tail.

Bird stones and boat stones were fetishes. Many of high polish or patina show great antiquity. One unusual fetish that we have represents a double pop-eyed bird stone, the lower portion of which is fashioned into a boat stone. It has two holes for suspension near the outer edge.

An unusual banded slate bird stone and conglomerate discoidal were found in a stonebox grave in Tennessee. It is now in our collection. Any student more than casually interested in bird stone fetishes should

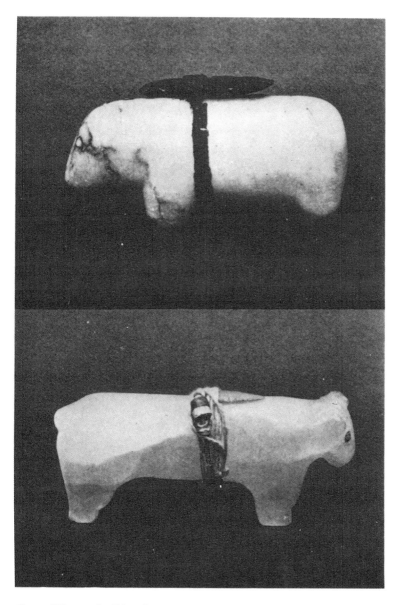

Top—Mountain Lion hunting fetish, Zuñi Pueblo, New Mexico
Bottom—Bear hunting fetish, Zuñi Pueblo, New Mexico

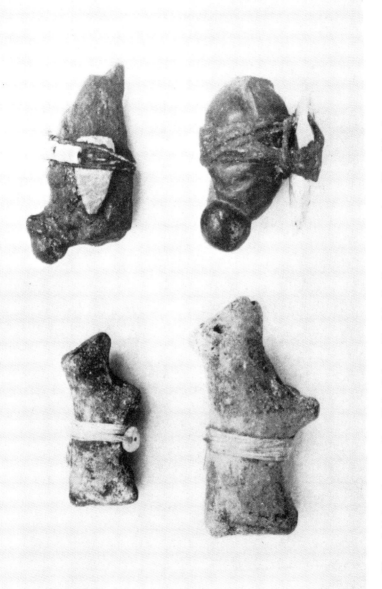

Left—Two fetishes from a "medicine" bag. Pueblo Indians, Acomita, New Mexico

Right, top—Hunting fetish of hematite representing an animal

Fetish made of hematite or iron ore, representing face with serpent outer edge—note eye of snake. In the King Collection

see the Joseph Ringeiser Jr. Collection in Wisconsin. He has amassed the most elaborate collection of bird stones known in the United States.

Boat stones were made out of granite, slate, and other material, to resemble canoes. They are highly polished, both inside and out. According to an old superstition, they were made to be destroyed. The shaman or medicine man wove incantations until the effigy was destroyed by fire, or water, similar to the old custom of making and burning effigies in the image of one responsible for misfortune. Two friends of mine amused me one time, as one had a mother-in-law who had caused her lots of trouble and the other had a step mother-in-law. Each decided to make an effigy in the mother-in-law's image and burn it.

We find quite a number of complete boat stones in our excavations and many are represented in various collections, such as Dr. George T. Heye's Collection at the Foundation for the American Indian in New York City and in the collection of the late Mr. Edward Payne.

The statement has been made that fetishes in the form of bird stones were worn on the brow by pregnant women. This might have been true among the pre-historic groups in Wisconsin and Michigan, where bird stones have been found in great quantities, but it is not true in the Mississippi Valley where I have excavated, as very few have been found. In seven years of excavating at the King Mounds we have not found one. We have a limited number, however, in our collection.

On the other hand, we have found a high proportion of infant remains, so the custom apparently was not used here. In my work as an ethnologist in Europe and in the Mississippi Valley for a number of years, I have come to the conclusion that fetishes and superstitious beliefs played an important part in the lives of prehistoric peoples. From my observation of dress and customs of the present day groups, fetishes and superstitions are still having a tremendous influence on the people today.

CHAPTER XI

FLINTS

MAN's existence on earth may be traced in almost all
countries by the relics of one of his most primitive
industries, the making of implements of stone. It is
probable that the use of wood may in many cases have
preceded that of stone, although from its perishable
nature not many examples have come down to us to
serve as evidence. Many wooden fragments, however,
have been found in the desert of Chinese Turkestan,
with inscriptions pertaining to the history of China.

There is a tradition among all ancient peoples that
the first inhabitants lived in caves. This remembrance
has been preserved among the Chinese and Egyptians.
From Plato we learn that Homer attributed that kind
of life to the savages of Sicily and Greece. Pliny speaks
of caves serving for houses among the Ethiopians and
other regions of Africa. Caves are also mentioned in
Scandinavian literature. So it is by cave contents that
we learn about prehistoric tribes.

The Stone Age lingers to this day among inhabitants in Northeastern Asia, the Indians of California
and the Rocky Mountains, the natives of New Caledonia and Andaman Islands, and some Australian
tribes.

In the Old World, however, with the exception of Northeastern Asia, history and tradition are silent as to implements of stone. In this field of research, the antiquity of stone implements must be determined by surrounding circumstances. The Hebrews mentioned stone knives in Exodus IV: 25 and Joshua V: 2, and other references to the use of stone may be found in Hebrew literature.

While implements of stone in many countries and various periods differ in form and skill of construction, throughout the entire world, from the earliest time to the present, there is a marvelous coincidence and curious resemblance, not merely in the simplest and most primitive, but also in the more complex types. Take, for example, an obsidian lance head, mounted on a staff, and an unmounted one of flint. One is still in use by the natives from the valley of Caledonia; the other came from the valley of the Somme, left by man when the Mammoth existed there and the river level was seventy feet above its present bed and had not cut out the broad valley through which it now flows.[30]

Another comparison is the implement used by the Eskimo for scraping skins, which is similar to those found in the Reindeer caves of France.

In China, archæology became a special branch of study in the Sung Dynasty. The special art of making rubbings of inscriptions on bronze and stone greatly facilitated the study of antiquities by scholars. In China, however, it is an immemorial tradition to regard the violation of tombs as highly immoral, and this tradition is very difficult to break. However, as this conception of the sacredness disappears, it will be possible to excavate such famous tombs as that of Confucius and his descendants at Chu Fou.[31] The Chinese people have great veneration for Confucius, so that not only his grave, but also those of his descendants have remained undisturbed. And as they are wonderful museums, containing the history of several thousand years, if the tombs are opened much will be learned about different periods of China.

Through the breaking of river banks caused by frequent inundations of the Yellow River, an old city was discovered, comparable to that of Pompeii. Old stone inscriptions of the Sung Dynasty were found. Customs, fashions, household utensils and handicrafts of that time were learned, as we are able to study folklore, customs and psychology of the aborigines from our excavations. The oldest stone inscription still in existence in China is the stone drum of the Chou Dynasty (827–788 B. C.).

Polished axes of greenstone have been found in India, England, South America, France, the Pacific and Solomon Islands; and when placed alongside the greenstone axes and celts of the Mound Builder, it is almost impossible to trace the source of origin.

One of the principal museums in Japan, having heard of the great amount of prehistoric material we are finding, sent us a quantity of their artifacts. On making comparisons, we were astonished at the similarity of the pottery and flint pieces.

Caves in the valley of Vézère in France yield many worked flints. Under peat bogs in Scotland and Ireland, stone and flint arrowheads were found in conjunction with animal bone and fragments of pottery. Blades of flint, discovered in English caves, are analogous to those found in France. In America, in mounds and ancient shell heaps of Georgia, California, and Florida, broken pottery and flint knives were unearthed, as well as pipes, arrowheads, axes and other ornaments of stone.

The whole region of Ohio and Kentucky is rich in remains of the old flint worker. After spring floods, fine specimens *in situ* are found projecting from the eroded banks or in the silt and gravel left by the falling river. Many are buried in its bed, to form, perchance, a subject of study for future generations, in the reconstructed river valleys of a new world.

In his volume, *Antiquity of Man,* Sir Arthur Keith states: "As the first gravel was being laid down, the culture of man was represented by flints, worked in a pre-Chellean style, and surprising pieces of bone work, and long before Piltdown days there had been the men who shaped eoliths."

On the barbs of the bone and flint implements of the Reindeer Age, grooves were thought to have been made to carry poison. The practice of smearing arrowheads with a poisonous substance to increase their destructive power has existed at all times and in all countries. The Tongouses of Nignaia Tongouska used the burnt flesh of the woodpecker, pounded and mixed with fat of any sort, except bear's fat (because that decomposed readily), and with this mixture, smeared their arrows used in hunting. In 1767, Gmelin in his *Voyage en Sibérie* wrote, "An animal struck with one of those always fell with the wound." Some harpoons were made with a single barb, while others had a number of barbs.

Hollowed pebbles of granite, quartzite, and sandstone were found in the caves at Les Éyzies and Périgord. Sometimes the flattening or hollow was very slight; other times it was deep enough to serve as a mortar. They appear to have been made by continued and repeated grinding with other hard substances. The surface was not polished and may have been used in grinding grain and other foods, or rubbing materials of paint, medicine, and poison. The suggestion is made that if they had been used in the preparation of red ocher or hematite there would still be faint traces of the reddish brown tint, but none show this discoloration.

The North American Indian used hollowed rock surfaces as mortars for grinding maize, as did the prehistoric cave-dwellers of France. They also have been reported from the Lake Dwellings of Switzerland. However, flat slabs, not pebbles, seem always to have been chosen for the cupped stones of Switzerland, as is still the case in Africa and elsewhere, according to F. Kellers, in his book, *Lake Dwellers of Switzerland,* page 25. No definite pestles were found with the mortar-like stones from the caves of Les Éyzies and La Madelaine in France; oval, flattish pebbles of quartz, worn on the edge, were found which may have been used. In the British Museum are stone mortars from Bruniguel. They are roughly dressed blocks of limestone, with a large shallow depression ground out of the surface. For one mortar a piece of mica was used as a pestle. Recently we excavated a large rectangular flat mortar, twelve by fourteen inches, with grooves on the edge for tool sharpening.

To make flint artifacts, flint was obtained with the fracture desired and free of flaws. Then these pieces were baked, steamed or annealed by placing them for about twenty-four hours in damp earth covered with a brisk fire. This is the belief of most authorities on the subject. With sharp blows they were broken into flakes, approximating the shape and size desired. For the more complete fashioning of the implement, a tool of the horn of mountain sheep, or the antler of deer or antelope was used. The flake of stone was held in one hand, placed on a little cushion made of untanned skin of some animal, to protect the hand from the flakes which were to be chipped off, and with a sudden pressure of the bone tool, the proper shape was obtained. The prehistoric artisan acquired great skill in this and the art was confined to but a few persons, who manu-

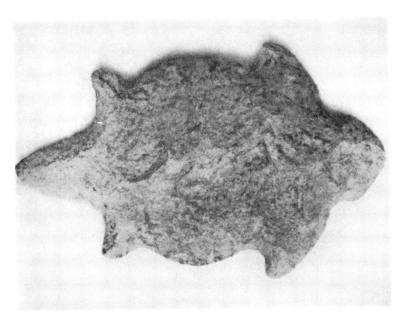

Flint turtle—a ceremonial or used as a fetish. In the King Collection. (From the Work Mounds, Tennessee)

Spear point, turkey-tail type, splendid workmanship. Thirty-one found in cache in Marshall County, Kentucky, now in King Collection

factured them for use and exchange in barter and trade.

The process of development of flint spear, arrow point or tool involved two operations. The primary stage developed the crude form from the nodule or piece of flint into a blank or form; secondary chipping reduced the blank or form into the finished article.

Flint occurs in sheets, seams, lumps, or nodules. Blows and pressure produce angular flakes with sharp edges which, when dressed into definite shape, were made into hammers, axes, drills, fish-hooks, wedges, celts, chisels, knives, scrapers, heads of spears, lances, hoes, discs, spades, javelins, harpoons and arrow points, reproducing all the forms common to the early Stone period of Europe and the Americas. Broken flint exposed to weather, water, and moisture underground suffers certain changes of surface. If dark-colored, it loses its uniform tint and translucency, becoming opaque and blotched, or a whitish-yellow color. Discoloration and patina, as well as the dendritic markings of metallic oxide of iron and carbonate of lime of permeating waters, cannot be taken as independent evidences of very great age for worked flints, since these superficial changes and appearances can be produced within limited periods of time. Nevertheless, it is necessary to recognize them as the result of some lapse of time and of certain conditions of deposit, as well as indications sometimes not only of the differences of faces provided artificially from natural surfaces of the flint, but of the successive production of artificial and accidental fractures in worked flints.[32] As an illustration of oxidation, in the remarkable copper find which we excavated not long ago there were a number of flint and stone objects, many of which were covered with copper oxide and patina.

In the Dordogne caves in France in the Reindeer Age, large, roughly chipped flint implements known as *"Langues de chat"* (not to be confused with the delicious pastry one buys in France of the same name) may have served to make holes in the ice during winter to spear the fish frequenting the great rivers at that time. The Eskimo, contemporary of the Stone Age and of the present time, employed analogous implements of stone for similar purposes. Even now in the Arctic regions, natives make holes in the ice and patiently wait for hours at the aperture until the seals, coming to the surface to breathe, can be struck and secured for food. The North American Indian employed similar weapons and tools.

In a mound in Ohio (Squier and Davis research), four thousand discs roughly prepared for future manufacture were found. They lay regularly, stacked edgewise in two layers. In another mound in Ohio, six thousand were found. Blocks of flint have occurred from time to time in Denmark, France and Belgium.

Flint might be compared to pig iron, ready to be turned to the special uses of the artificer for barter and trade. At different stone periods flint was disseminated from countries where native flint occurred during intertribal relations, just as in the late copper and bronze periods of Europe, those prized metals were diffused through remote areas. Possibly they were deposited in sepulchral mounds to furnish the dead materials from which to fashion implements adapted to the new life on which they were about to enter.

Around the pits of Flint Ridge, Ohio, may be seen the accumulated result of centuries of mining and quarrying, extending in all probability from the era of the Mound Builder to the extinction or removal of the Miamis, Shawnees, and other historic Indian occupancy of the Ohio Valley. Swept by floods into the lower valleys, smaller fragments of flint would disappear; other specimens survived unchanged, as those found in the valley of the Somme, which startle archæologists by their quantity.

Tools in use with the old cave-folk in Europe and the Americas were used in the ordinary work of flaying, cutting, scraping and carving. Some of the implements bear significant or individual marks of ownership. Implements found in a cave at Le Moustier in France had sharp hatchet-like edges, usually curved along one margin, retaining some portion of the original flint nodule.

A general and well-founded idea prevails that the old Mound Builder, in the manner of the modern Indian, was in the habit of making caches of flint rocks and nodules, so as to protect the material from exposure and the atmosphere. Stone knives could be hafted with a handle of cord and fur, like those used in Australia.

New finds are reported as time goes on. I was interested in the tooth of an extinct type of horse found in a seam in the fluorspar mines in Rosiclare, Illinois. Figures of animals engraved or sculptured on stone, bone and reindeer horn have appeared at Les Éyzies, Laugerie Basse and La Madelaine. Le Moustier cave had many worked flints, but no engraved or sculptured animal figures. Near Mentone, flints, in association with other objects, were found with Cro-Magnon burials. Some of the horse illustrations are badly drawn but nevertheless convey the illustration very well, and are crude attempts to represent contemporary life.

Harpoons, barbed on one or both edges, were found in caves of Périgord and used probably for salmon fishing, like those employed by North American Indians.

Sandstone, with grooves deep and narrow to fit implements, was used in rounding and sharpening splinters of bone for needles, awls, and flint arrowheads.

Recently, under the direction of Dr. John B. Ruyle, President of the Illinois Archæological Society, a prehistoric find was made in central Illinois. Human remains, in association with a copper spear and animal bones, were found and should prove a source of information when the work is completed.

Almost every collector has a number of fine flints, as flint in some form is a favorite item. Mr. Frank Aldrich, of Bloomington, Illinois, has one of the finest caches of semi-translucent white flint, made in leaf-shaped notched spear points, that I have ever seen. In the Jefferson Museum in Saint Louis, Missouri, is the famous cache of forty-six magnificently chipped ceremonials of maces, scepters, swords, discs and a flint turtle, from Humphreys County, Tennessee, not far from the Harpeth River mounds.

In the King collection there is a cache of thirty-one turkey tail, notched spear points, five to seven inches in length, beautifully chipped of nodule flint, as thin as a knife blade. Wonderful workmanship, all made by the same artisan, comparable to the finest of the Solutrean flint work of Europe. Another cache from Camden Landing, Tennessee River, Tennessee, was obtained from Dr. McQuarry. They are of translucent white flint and made by a master craftsman. Ceremonial flints found in California are very similar to the beautiful ceremonials excavated in Tennessee.

It has been possible in the rich bottom lands of the Mississippi and Ohio Valleys to assemble the greatest cross-section of chipped flints, gouges, celts, hoes, spades, drills, and points to be found anywhere, and these are now in the King collection. Some of the flint ceremonial caches are magnificently chipped of lustrous black flint—discs, poniards, scepters, and maces which taper to a sharp rim, the thinness of a knife blade; one of the finest chipped flint turtles to be seen in this country; beautiful spear points in all sizes and shapes, some with serrated and beveled edges; tang, bird and war points scarcely half an inch in length. The chipped flint spades and hoes are highly polished on the edges from long usage in agricultural pursuits, and are also of various shapes and sizes. Many of the flints show exquisite delicacy and some elaborately finished blades of various forms surpass those of the European Neolithic period.

Of the many artifacts of prehistoric man, I believe I like the flints best. The translucency, the musical tone when they clink together, and the feel of the superbly chipped surfaces give me a feeling of deep satisfaction and the greatest of admiration for an art born in the dusky recesses of the Stone Age.

CHAPTER XII

FIRE

WE accept the great comfort derived from fire as we accept many things; until we are without it, we don't realize how important it is to our well-being. Fire is made by various means, by friction and by spontaneous combustion.

North of the Timagami region in Canada, I have seen guides, while on fishing trips, experiment in making fire without matches, by twirling a round stick very rapidly into the hollow of a flat piece of cedar. Sparks would soon ignite the frayed bark underneath.

It is fortunate that Boy Scouts are taught fire making today. How different the story of the ship-wrecked cab driver might have been on Galapàgos, which is dramatically told in William Beebe's *Galapàgos*. For several months some sailors were shipwrecked on this island. There was no fresh water and no matches. Tragedy and death were stalking all around. One day, when they were completely without hope and thought it was the end, the cook from the boat took off his shirt. In the words of the narrator, "Well, sir, that cook had had a box of matches squashed flat in his underneath shirt pocket for two months and a half, and us living on raw turtle. Can you beat it?

"Some of them matches was damp, and talk about nursing! Baby! we laid them out in a row on a rock in the sun and we built a little wall of rocks around 'em and then we all sat around and watched them dry. Once in a while someone would reach out and turn one over when he thought one side was done."

We Americans require more heat in our houses than Europeans. One summer in Scotland, I spent a night in a hotel where it was impossible to get a fire. I was so cold that I went to bed with everything on, including a long heavy Scotch suède coat, shoes and hat, and even then I nearly froze.

With primitive peoples, ignorance of fire must have been noted first when the season changed. The Eskimo was not as dependent on fire as the Mound Builder. He ate blubber and his fur garments kept him warm. Even now he uses it more for protection from insects than anything else, as the negroes burn rags to keep away the mosquitoes. Steatite or soapstone lamps were used to melt snow for drinking water and furnished a limited amount of heat for the Eskimos.

Various methods were used in making fire without matches, such as rubbing two dry sticks together. A piece of quartz or iron pyrite, rubbed against a piece of flint stone, would make sparks that would ignite any dry frayed moss or grass.

Tecumseh, of the historic Indian, in an eloquent warning to his tribe to resist the deadly encroachments of the White Man, told them to throw away their fire

Deville

Eagle Bowl excavated in Burial Tombs at King Mounds

steels and awaken the sleeping flame as their fathers once did, and to throw their clothing away and put on skins won by hunting, if they would escape the anger of the Great Spirit.

We have many cultures here at the King Mounds excavations similar to the Mexican people. A plumed eagle bowl that we excavated shows Central American influence. I am inclined to think that the premeditated burnings here are comparable also to the burnings of the fifty-two year cycle in Mexico.

In Mexico the fire god was venerated as the father of gods. In *The Sun, the Moon, and a Rabbit,* Amelia Martinez Del Rio has written an interesting story about this god. He was called Hue-hue-te-otl, which means "The Oldest God," and was created by the friction of a stone knife falling from the heavens to the earth. He taught the people to make fire by the friction of two sticks. He then made the fire bright by blowing on it. People received this precious gift with great joy and kept it carefully in their homes as one of their greatest treasures. He was greatly loved and on this altar incense was burned and turtledoves sacrificed. Old men and old women were especially devoted to this father of the gods, and they made him offerings of jars of the wine of the cactus plant. This pleased the god very much, as he was fond of this wine. In front of every temple, two enormous fires were kept burning day and night, and to honor the father of the gods the people began the fifty-two year cycle, with the festival of the "New Fire."

In Teotihuacán are two great pyramids, the Temple of the Sun and the Temple of the Moon, which men toiled years and years to complete. It was necessary to carry the material in baskets on their backs. The pyramid of the Sun was painted dark red and decorated with hundreds of tiger heads in different colors. Opposite the stairway on two smaller pyramids were two enormous braziers where the cycle fires burned continuously day and night for fifty-two years, the duration of the cycle.

The world was supposed to come to an end at this time, and the people fasted for five days and burned all their dwellings. When the world didn't come to an end, they were agreeably surprised and the priest started a new fire on top of one of the pyramids by rubbing two stone knives together. It is by reading the kitchen midden of the burning of the fifty-two year cycle that archæologists are able to date ruins in Mexico today. A great celebration was held at the kindling of the new fires in thanksgiving for another fifty-two years. There are many legends woven around fire, and the following is the Mexican legend known as the "Sun of Fire":

"Many centuries had gone by. Men and women were wicked. They lied. They gossiped. They were thieves. And they forgot to say their prayers. The gods held a meeting in heaven to decide what should be done. This time they sent the god of Fire to punish mankind. In the city of Teotihuacán there lived a newly married couple. One evening, this man and woman sat by the fire of their hearth and gazed into the flames, as they talked in a low voice of their love and of their many dreams. Suddenly from the flames sprang an old and wrinkled man, who told them that a terrible disaster would afflict mankind. He said that volcanoes would vomit rivers of lava and that a devastating fire would rain from the sky. The wrinkled old god said: 'All mankind but you two shall perish. Take with you the fire of your hearth and hide in yonder cave. The gods love you because of your faithfulness, and will save you so that mankind will not disappear.' Then the old man vanished and the couple hastened to the cave, taking with them the fire of their hearth. S· ddenly, the mountains vomited lava and flames raised from the sky. The inhabitants of the earth remembered their gods, and in tears and sorrow they prayed, 'Oh, gods, that we were birds.' And the gods in pity granted their prayer. Millions of birds filled the skies, soaring above the flaming earth. Only one couple was saved, and they hid in a cave and watched over the fire of their hearth." [33]

A short distance from Mexico City are the ruins of Pedregal, a site where lava flow covered an entire district. Burials with their possessions may be seen. It reminded me of the foregoing legend when I saw it.

Fire has played an important role all through the ages in ceremonials. It is symbolical. Today we have the perpetual fire in memory of the Unknown Soldier which burns under the Arc de Triomphe in Paris.

Sacrifices by fire were practiced as an important and oft-repeated part of the sacred rites of the Mound Builder. We find many instances of premeditated burnings in our excavations, altar fires having been quenched by dirt being thrown over the fire while glowing in repeated sacrificial rites. This fortunately preserved them for future study.

The prehistoric inhabitants weren't the only ones to have ceremonials. We have our great ceremonials today, as illustrated recently in the coronation of the present Pope in Rome. It is always a wonder to me how great crowds can be silent. At the dedication of a large stadium, shortly after the war, seventy-five thousand people were so silent and reverent at the playing of "taps" that not a sound could be heard, save the clicking of the telegraph keys in the distance. Another time, an even larger group of people were massed in the square around Notre Dame in Paris where great flood lights had been placed to illuminate the Cathedral for the first time. We all stood in anticipation of the event. When the lights were turned on the startled doves flew madly about, the statues of the saints appeared to be shocked, and even the gargoyles seemed to have an expression of surprise. Personally, I didn't like it. It was as if the veil of centuries had been rudely torn aside. Too much light destroys illusions.

In prehistoric times, the shaman or priest was the

important figure. Among the historic Indians, the medicine man was greatly respected. I was interested in a talk a Thlinkit Indian from Alaska gave not long ago at one of our universities. He spoke of their ceremonials and the power of the medicine man even now. Totem poles in his part of the country were legendary, burial, and ceremonial. The old chief was the ruler of the clan and sometimes he would have live slaves buried under a totem pole. The last of the tribal officers to go were the chief and the medicine man. The medicine man was not only the doctor, but the prophet as well, and he played an important part in the life of the Indian.

This young man, when a boy, often fell into the sea while playing with a little boat. His mother took him to the medicine man, who told her that the spirit above the boy was restless. He then took the boy into his shelter, which was filled with odors of stale food, and went into a trance for five minutes over a glass of water. When he came to, he advised the boy to stay away from water for ten days. The mother paid the medicine man an amount equal to ten dollars. The more the medicine man received, the better chance one had of getting well.

Indian boys in that part of Alaska are given to their uncle for training in woodcraft and out-of-door life. The parents plan all marriages, and a member of the Eagle clan, for example, must marry into another clan such as the Raven. This is very much like old prehistoric customs.

Ceremonial dances which must have been handed down through the centuries are used by the historic Indians. One time, accompanied by my family, I attended a ceremonial dance of the Indians in the Lac du Flambeau region in Wisconsin. When the young chief, bowing low, his great feathers sweeping the ground, asked me to dance, I refused politely. Afterwards, I was annoyed with myself for not joining the circle, as the beat of the tom-toms was very fascinating; and with the family taking moving pictures, it would have been interesting in after years. The squaws had a solitary dance by themselves and seemed to enjoy it, although there was no change of expression on their faces.

In one of our excavations we uncovered a burned area of prehistoric corn kernels, six feet in diameter. Thirty thousand kernels were taken from the spot. Evidently it had been a corn ceremonial, as dirt had been thrown on it in the course of the burning.

The premeditated burnings here of altars and house sites might be traced to two sources. From the habit of burying the littlest children within the house, illness was bound to occur from the poor sanitation. If we had the same custom of burying our dead within the home, we, too, should be ill. However, in the superstitious, ignorant mind of the aboriginal peoples, they doubtless thought their gods were angered when the children died, and they burned their buildings to appease the wrath of the gods. Fire purifies and naturally their health was much better; but they, no doubt, thought it was because this wrath had been appeased. On the other hand, the premeditated burnings may have been the fifty-two year cycle burnings of Mexico, since we find there were many cultures in common.

According to an old Cherokee myth, "In the beginning there was no fire, and the world was cold, until the Thunders (Ani'-hyun'-tikwalaski), who lived up in Galunlati, sent their lightning and put fire into the bottom of a hollow sycamore tree which grew on an island.

"The animals knew it was there, because they could see the smoke coming out at the top, but they could not get to it on account of the water, so they held a council to decide what to do. This was a long time ago.

"Every animal that could fly or swim was anxious to go after the fire. The Raven offered, and because he was so large and strong they thought he could surely do the work, so he was sent first. He flew high and far across the water and alighted on the sycamore tree, but while he was wondering what to do next, the heat had scorched all his feathers black, and he was frightened and came back without the fire.

"The little Screech-owl (Wahuhu) volunteered to go, and reached the place safely, but while he was looking down into the hollow tree a blast of hot air came up and nearly burned out his eyes. He managed to fly home as best he could, but it was a long time before he could see well, and his eyes are red to this day.

"Then the Hooting Owl (Uguku) and the Horned Owl (Tskili) went, but by the time they got to the hollow tree the fire was burning so fiercely that the smoke nearly blinded them, and the ashes carried up by the wind made white rings about their eyes. They had to come home again without the fire, but with all their rubbing they were never able to get rid of the white rings.

"Now no more of the birds would venture, and so little Uksuhi snake, the black racer, said he would go through water and bring back some fire. He swam across to the island and crawled through the grass to the tree, and went in by a small hole at the bottom. The heat and smoke were too much for him, too, and after dodging about blindly over hot ashes, until he was almost on fire himself, he managed by good luck to get out again at the same hole, but his body had been scorched black, and he has ever since had the habit of darting and doubling on his track as if trying to escape from close quarters.

"He came back, and the great blacksnake, Gulegi, 'The Climber,' offered to go for fire. He swam over to the island and climbed up the tree on the outside, as the blacksnake always does, but when he put his head down into the hole the smoke choked him so that he fell into the burning stump, and before he could climb out again he was as black as Uksuhi.

"Now they held another council, for still there was no fire and the world was cold, but birds, snakes, and four-footed animals, all had some excuse for not going, because they were all afraid to venture near the burning sycamore, until at last Kanaaneski Amaiyehi (the Water Spider) said she would go.

"This is not the water spider that looks like a mosquito, but the other one, with black downy hair and red stripes on her body. She can run on top of water or dive to the bottom, so there would be no trouble to get over to the island, but the question was, how could she bring back the fire? 'I'll manage that,' said the Water Spider; so she spun a thread from her body and wove it into a tusti bowl, which she fastened on her back. Then she crossed over to the island and through the grass to where the fire was still burning. She put one little coal of fire into her bowl, and came back with it, and ever since we have had fire, and the Water Spider still keeps her tusti bowl." [34]

According to some legends, it was the fox who stole the fire by wrapping cedar bark around his tail and thrusting it into the blaze while dancing. Another myth insists that it was a rabbit who brought back the fire. Pretending to bow low at the dance before the flame, he lighted sticks of rosin concealed on his head.

The historic Indian's heaven was called the Happy Hunting Ground. A favorite story concerns an Indian who became a Christian. When he died he went to the White Man's heaven, but he was most unhappy there. Everyone had relatives to visit with but himself; there were no ancestors waiting for him, no hunting, no fishing nor any of the occupations in which he was wont to delight. Finally, the Great Manitou called him and asked why he was so unhappy in his beautiful heaven, and the Indian replied that he missed the association of his own people. So the Great Manitou told him he couldn't send him to the Indian heaven as he had chosen the other one, but since he had been a very good man he would send him back to earth again.

The historic Indian also believed that sacred fires still burned in the ancient mounds of their forefathers. During the Civil War superstitious soldiers swore that they saw the smoke from these hidden fires.

Romans kindled sacred fires and the Mound Builder erected mounds on the highest hills, built large fires, kept them burning for long periods, or renewed them at frequent intervals. The great burned areas show marks of intense heat. Oftentimes the burned area was two feet deep, the fires having been used, no doubt, as ancient signal stations. They are still in use by remote native tribes who send up columns of smoke as a warning that the enemy is at hand, like the old signal fires of the Indian.

Beautiful ornaments of pearl, copper, and shell have felt the destructive flame of fire but the altars are still preserved, with a few offerings on them. Mica was used very often to ignite fire on the sacred altar. It is fortunate that pottery is not affected seriously by fire, otherwise the complete record of the textiles would have been lost.

FIRE

We don't see fire as often as the aboriginal peoples, for our heat comes indirectly from furnaces in the majority of homes. But the prehistoric man sat around the fire all year through and noticed the flames—fire worship was only a step removed from his daily life.

CHAPTER XIII

COPPER

SECRECY, resulting from the valuable finds and superstitions, concealed the source of copper from the White Man for many years, according to old Jesuit records.

The Mound Builder knew the use and source of copper, and possessed a slightly higher metallurgic knowledge than the Indian hunter of the North, as demonstrated by his ability in other fields and by the great earthworks from which his name is derived.

He was not advanced so far in civilization as the peoples of Mexico or Central America, as his social and intellectual development was rudimentary; however, he was greatly in advance of the Indian hunter or ancient copper miner.

By portages with his light birch bark canoe, from the Mississippi River through Lake Huron and Ottawa into the Saint Lawrence region, and by Lakes Huron, Erie, and Ontario into the Hudson, he could traverse the waterways to the source of the Trappean rocks in Isle Royale of the Lake Superior region.

Copper was an object of barter and trade and consequently was a great stimulus to commerce. It was diffused by primitive commercial exchanges, through the vast regions watered by the Mississippi and Ohio Rivers and their great tributaries, including the Atlantic states and the shores of the Great Lakes.

Other countries, like Egypt, Peru, Greece and Mexico, had quantities of gold and silver to make ornaments and tools, but copper was nearly, if not actually, the most valuable metal the Mound Builder possessed.

Ornaments and tools were wrought from virgin copper, by means of the hammer, without smelting, alloy, or the use of fire. However, fire was an invaluable aid in reducing and smelting the ore.

In Cornwall and Wales, copper has been mined since the early ages. It is found in many sections of Mexico, some in New Mexico, Arizona, and in various other parts of the Americas. However, the richest source is in the Lake Superior and Isle Royale districts, where it was found in the pure metallic state in great masses. It was malleable and could be hammered. Hundreds of tons were mined. In Cornwall, Wales and Devon, England, copper is mined from ores.

I always had a suppressed desire to see Mount Snowdon in Wales, and one day with my family, we started there from London. It happened to be a bank holiday, and consequently a day when travel was almost impossible because of the surging crowds. In spite of this, we finally arrived at Llandudno, where we were forced to spend the night, as it was too late to get the train to Mount Snowdon.

Llandudno proved to be a beautiful and exclusive watering place. In the evening we were fortunate to secure tickets for a lovely concert. In the midst of a singing of the beautiful *Suicidio* aria from Ponchielli's *La Gioconda,* accompanied by a sixty-piece orchestra, I was completely entranced, but in my subconscious mind I was aware that an old sea captain turned around and gave me a terrible look. However, the charm of the music held me enthralled and I paid no attention to anything else. After the song was finished, the old man turned around again and glowered at me, but still I thought, "Oh, well, it is a foreign country and people have strange ways." Then the singer started another beautiful aria, in the midst of which the old man's daughter turned around and gave me a meaning glance. By that time my family looked at me as much as to say, "What are you doing?" Upon investigating, I found that I was pulling the old man's coat tail and pinching his *"derrière"* with my foot in the crack of his seat.

The seats were large and of red velvet, but the old man was quite plump and filled all the space. I have a bad habit of putting my toe in the seat in front of me. I had made myself quite comfortable! During the intermission the conservative ladies, with their best "Queen Mary" hats, eyed me with stern disapproval for annoying the old sea salt. My embarrassment was intense!

Some day I hope to return to Llandudno and spend

a week there, for it is a beautiful spot at the tipmost part of Wales, unless it has changed as most things do. Like Brittany, twilight does not descend until after ten o'clock. The charming little hotel was delightful, with its delicious food and fine old linens.

The next day we went to Mount Snowdon and had to change trains twice during the journey. While waiting for one of the trains, we visited the mines where copper has been found for centuries.

In 1850, in the copper mines at Llandudno, Carnarvanshire, chisels, picks of bronze, stone mauls and axes were excavated which must have been used to detach the ore from the rock. They were thought to belong to the period prior to the Roman occupation in Great Britain. It is said the old mining tools used by these peoples are similar to those found in the Isle Royale district, proving that minds correspond and human ingenuity is the same the world over.

In 1666, the Jesuit father Claude Alloüez, visited La Pointe, on the shores of which lived hundreds of the historic Chippewa Indians. He reported: "The savages reverence the lake as a divinity and offer sacrifices to it because of the great size, for it is two hundred leagues long and eighty broad; and also because of the abundance of fish it supplies to them in lieu of game, which is scarce in the environs. They often find in the lake pieces of copper weighing ten to twelve pounds.

"I have seen many such pieces in the hands of savages; and as they are superstitious they regard them as divinities, or as gifts which the gods who dwell beneath the waters have bestowed on them to promote their welfare; hence they preserve such pieces of copper wrapped up along with their most prized possessions.

"By some they have been preserved upwards of fifty years and others have had them in their families from time immemorial, cherishing them as their household gods.

"There was visible for some time near the shore, a large rock made entirely of copper—with its top rising above the water, which afforded an opportunity for those passing to cut pieces from it. But when I passed in the vicinity, nothing could be seen of it. I believe that the storms, which are very frequent, and as violent as on the ocean, had covered the rock with sand. Our Indians wished to persuade me it was a divinity which had disappeared, but for what reason they would not say." [35]

Copper and stone implements of the miners were found; also wooden tools, bowls, miners' shovels, and stone mauls like our stone axes. In an ancient trench, a solid copper mass weighing two to three tons was recovered in 1874; it lay seventeen feet below the surface. Stone mauls and hammers weighing ten to thirty pounds lay scattered near by.

The abandoned tools of the copper miners still remain in some of the old trenches, where trees have grown that are hundreds of years old. The filling of

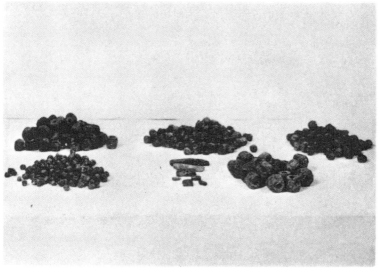

Kentucky copper finds at King Mounds

the trenches with vegetable soil must have been the work of centuries.

It has been suggested that since no house sites of the old copper miners in the Lake Superior region have ever been excavated, they may have worked the mines only in the summer time, leaving when winter came and returning in the spring. However, that is conjecture.

To travel hundreds of miles in frail boats loaded with copper required enterprise. But prehistoric peoples and pioneers of all races have been sturdy and adventurous, so such travel is not improbable. However, I do not feel it is the correct solution to the disappearance of the copper miner. Perhaps devastating pestilence caused them to vanish, or the invasion of some barbaric race, or the shadows of the evening may have told them their work was finished.

Articles made from copper, such as axes, chisels, gauges, knives, and spear heads similar to bayonets, have been found in mounds. Copper was also used for bracelets and other ornaments, rudely wrought with the hammer.

In Mexico, Peru, and Central America the people knew the use of the crucible and furnace. Metallurgic arts were developed extensively, but the Mound Builder had not advanced to that degree in his knowledge of metallurgy.

An interesting story by Father Dablon, a Jesuit, illustrates the highly superstitious nature of the Indian. He recorded, in 1667, a marvelous account communicated to him by four Indians who in olden times, before the coming of the French, lost their way in a fog but finally landed on an island. They cooked their meals in Indian fashion by heaping stones and casting them in a birch-bark pail filled with water. The stones proved to be lumps of copper, which they carried off with them; but they had hardly left the shore when a loud and angry voice asked, "What thieves are those that carry off my children's cradles and playthings?"

One of the Indians died immediately from fear; two others died soon after; while the fourth survived only long enough to reach home and relate what had happened. They had, no doubt, been poisoned by the copper used in the cooking. Ever after the Indians steered their course far off the site of the haunted island. Father Dablon also reported that he was presented with pieces of copper weighing twenty to one hundred pounds which had been found by the squaws when digging holes to plant their corn.

Beautiful copper has been found in the Hopewell Culture Mounds in Ohio under the direction of Dr. William C. Mills, one of the pioneer archæologists, and his able successor, Director Henry Clyde Shetrone, of the Ohio Museum, Columbus, Ohio. Dr. Warren K. Morehead also found copper in Ohio and in the Etowah-Tomlin Site, Cartersville, Georgia. On July 19, 1819, Dr. S. P. Hildreth, of Marietta, Ohio, wrote a letter describing copper, silver, and iron ore ornaments found in a mound located in one of the streets of Marietta.

In the Great Lakes district, copper is very common; it was used for utilitarian purposes by the early inhabitants. Here in the Mississippi Valley it was precious, because it had to be brought in by trade and commerce, or by a long journey.

At Easter time in 1938, we excavated a small mound near Wickliffe, Kentucky, and found the greatest find of solid copper large beads that has ever been excavated in this region, again proving that it isn't the largest mounds that contain the most artifacts. It is generally the very small mounds that yield the treasures.

Following are the notes on the copper find that I wrote the day of the excavation:

"Handfuls of copper jewels—solid copper beads and axes—pounds and pounds of copper—the greatest copper find ever made in Kentucky, and which had lain in the earth hundreds of years, in the burial of a great shaman or leader of the Mound Builders, in a small mound overlooking the Mississippi River a short distance from the King Mounds in Wickliffe, Kentucky.

"A few days ago we were told of a remarkable find in a mound a short distance away. Accompanied by my husband, Colonel Fain White King, archæologist, I immediately went down to the mound to see if I could secure some ethnological data. Fortunately for science and archæology, the disturbance was slight, so we made arrangements to bring our trained organization down at once to interpret the archæological and ethnological story. We surveyed and laid out the mound in the usual five-foot square method of excavating, which we have used during the past several years.

"The mound combined a pit and mound burial and contained only one male burial. The burial was placed directly on the clay at the bottom of the pit; then the mound built over it. It was an entirely different burial from the ones we have excavated the last few years in this district. The others had charcoal under and over the burials in the majority of cases; consequently the skeletal material was in an excellent state of preservation. The skeletal material here, however, was poorly preserved, due to the absence of charcoal under the burial which would have neutralized the acids of the earth. Only portions of the burial in contact with the copper oxidation were preserved; the remainder of the skeletal material was indicated by white streaks in the earth, all that was left of this old Mound Builder. Abstraction or wear of the teeth indicated he was of venerable age.

"The length of the pit was seven feet, five inches; the depth four feet, eight inches at the deepest part. Charcoal was used in a strikingly different manner in this burial, and what appears to be the inner bark or part of a tree was woven like the bottom of a wicker chair. It was eleven inches wide and seemed to form the entrance of the pit in a strip eight feet long and eleven inches wide. One wonders if these Mound Builders were fire worshipers.

"Apparently when they had finished the burial pit, the strip of woven material was placed from the top of the pit to the bottom, on both sides, at the feet of the burial. Prior to replacing the dirt in the pit, this strip was burned, and while it was burning, dirt was thrown onto the ceremonial offering, reducing it into charcoal instead of white wood ashes, which would have occurred if it had not been a premeditated burning, indicating possible fire worship.

"Six hundred and nineteen solid copper beads graduated in size from three and one-half inches in circumference to one-half inch; five solid copper axes, ranging from six and three-quarter inches to three-quarters of an inch in length; six elongated beads, from three inches in length to one inch; one green stone celt; four chipped flint celts; two nodule flint spear points, five-sixths of an inch in length; eleven nodule arrow points; and three chip scrapers comprised the find. The flints were at the feet, the axes at his hand, and the beads on his breast. Due to the oxidation of the copper, the string or thong upon which the beads were strung is still preserved. Palæobotanical research will reveal, no doubt, the kind of material used.

"An amusing incident occurred here. The farmer was so thrilled when he found the beads that he thought he had discovered a hoard of gold nuggets. He hastened to the village to have one of the beads cut in half and tested. What a disappointment to him—only copper! But what a thrill to us! Solid copper, the greatest archæological copper find ever made in Kentucky and one of the most remarkable copper finds in the United States, north of Mexico. Some of the other interesting finds are from the Hopewell Culture Mounds in Ohio, the mound in Spiro, Oklahoma, and the Etowah-Tomlin Mounds in Georgia. Copper has been found in Kentucky before, but never in such a large quantity. Most of the copper originated from the Lake Superior region, especially the Isle Royale locality, where it was mined over a long period of time by the aboriginal peoples. What a story—copper from the Lake Superior district now in a mound in Kentucky—and what labor the mining involved!

"Western Kentucky contains some of the richest undeveloped prehistoric mounds and sites in the Mississippi Valley. Under a cliff near the river we secured a cache of thirty-one turkey tail notched spear-points, five inches to seven inches in length, magnificently chipped of nodule flint, as thin as a knife blade. Wonderful workmanship by the same artisan, comparable to the fine flints made in Europe by prehistoric peoples.

"Tired, sunburned, disheveled—but happy. Vale, Mound Builder. Civilization and the plow had almost obliterated your resting place. Now your beautiful copper will reflect great honor and dignity on your race for generations to come:

COPPER

'O to mount again where erst I haunted;
Where the old red hills are bird-enchanted,
And the low green meadows
   Bright with sward;
And when even dies, the million-tinted,
And the night has come, and planets glinted.
Lo! the valley hollow,
Lamp-bestarred.

   O to dream, O to awake and wander
There, and with delight to take and render,
Through the trance of silence,
   Quiet breath.
Lo! for there, among the flowers and grasses,
Only the mightier movements sounds and passes;
Only winds and rivers,
   Life and death.' " [36]

CHAPTER XIV

PIPES AND BANNER STONES

JUDGING from the great number of pipes one sees in various collections, the aborigines must have been inveterate smokers or used tobacco extensively in their ceremonials. These pipes are made out of various materials, such as clay, stone, porphyry, jasper, steatite, and serpentine, a beautiful semi-translucent mineral.

Steatite or soapstone was used because it is not fragile, is easily carved and can endure great heat. It comes principally from North Carolina. The pipes are in many forms—tubular, elbow, disc, platform, conical, rectangular, and human, animal, bird, frog, fish, and reptile effigy types. Extraordinary care was lavished on the carvings of pipes. The majority are delicately wrought and highly polished. "Some of the portrait or human head effigies are unsurpassed by any specimens of ancient American art, not excepting the best productions of Mexico and Peru." [37]

There is one small squirrel pipe, exquisitely carved, in my collection, and a replica of a bear. Another made out of Indiana limestone is an inverted owl which, in order to be smoked, must be held upside down. Back of the head there is a hole filled with a copper ring so that it could be suspended around the neck. Another

[152]

handsome one of brown pottery is an effigy of a man, crouching on his feet, with the bowl of the pipe between his legs. A unique one represents a quartzite frog with a plummet in the bowl at the top of his head. The ingenious aborigine who made this pipe had a piece of jewelry or plummet to hang around his neck as well as a pipe. It has been suggested, since the plummet was made of the same material as the pipe and was found with it, that it was purposely used to extinguish the burning tobacco in the pipe and served in some ceremonial capacity. Various mounds have yielded beautiful pipes; especially fine ones were recovered from the Etowah-Tomlin Mounds in Cartersville, Georgia.

In 1901, Dr. William C. Mills excavated a human effigy pipe in the Adena Mound in Scioto Valley, Ohio, showing ear spools and elaborate hairdress. This effigy illustrates the nude body with only a loin cloth, typical dress of the Mound Builder. The top of the headdress was the mouthpiece and the bowl was between the feet.

After a storm which uprooted several trees, a beautifully polished stone human effigy pipe was uncovered in a mound on the old battle field at Shiloh, Tennessee. It represents a female in a crouching position, and for workmanship and size is one of the finest pipes that has ever been found. It may be seen in the Museum at the Shiloh National Park.

Recently we secured a pottery pipe with three holes in the bottom of the bowl. The bowl and stem of this pipe were made separately, then joined as a unit. Three holes permitted the smoke from the burning tobacco to be drawn into the mouth and allowed the nicotine and loose tobacco to be retained in the bowl of the pipe. From the published records on pipes and the available material that we have for research, this appears to be the only pipe of this type. Many advertisements of pipes illustrate that certain patented ones are made to keep the nicotine and tobacco from the mouth. The artisan Mound Builder who made this pipe should have had his original idea patented. In Ohio, two hundred pipes were found in one mound.

A paper written for Congrès International des Americanistes, 1877, states: "The red pipestone of Minnesota was unknown to the Mound Builder, but in the last century pipes made of it were not uncommon in the Ohio Valley a thousand miles from the quarry." Our excavations have proven this statement to be false, as we have excavated pipestone from prehistoric mounds. At McClouds Bluff, twenty miles south of Wickliffe, Kentucky, red and gray pipestone, worked into pipes, has been excavated in prehistoric mounds.

The pipe was associated with solemn and religious rites and ceremonials, both in ancient and modern times. It played a very prominent part in the life of the Mound Builder and still retains its place among the paraphernalia of the medicine man or priest of the historic Indian, as well as giving pleasure and enjoyment

[154]

to modern man, whether the pipe is of the corn cob variety or the most expensive imported one.

BANNER STONES

The use of banner stones has never been definitely understood. Clarence B. Moore found a number on Green River in Kentucky and gave them the name of net spacers, as he found them in conjunction with bone-weaving tools. However, this opinion is not generally held by archæologists.

I have often visualized banner stones, which always have a hole through them, as fitted with a handle or staff, beautifully decorated with feathers and streamers of many colors, in the hand of a shaman, as a symbol of authority or power, making braves, leaders, or minor officials, and possibly performing marriage rites, if there were such customs.

Banner stones show great skill on the part of the artisan and are particularly beautiful in different colors of quartz and other brilliant stones. Some of them are very handsome and in such excellent condition that they seem indicative of regalia, handed down from generation to generation as ceremonial objects. Banner stones occur in diversified and unusual forms— hour glass, saddle back, cross, pick, butterfly, and human effigy types.

There is a myth that the butterfly type of banner stone represents the Thunder Bird, a mythological creature who was revered by the prehistoric peoples. It was supposed to have been carried on a pole similar to our flag pole, or attached to the prow of the canoe or pirogue.

Mr. Byron Knoblock, of La Grange, Illinois, is considered an authority on the banner stone, and is now assembling material showing the types, kinds, and variations in a detailed analysis.

CHAPTER XV

BONE IMPLEMENTS

LIKE the words of Handel's beautiful aria from *Semele*, "Where'er ye walk" at the King Mounds are discarded, misplaced, and deposited artifacts.

Not long ago I had one of the workers plant a peach tree, and two feet down the spade upturned a long, tapering, highly-polished bone needle and two pieces of pottery. Two weeks later, while we were doing some landscaping, a cache of chipped flint cane knives, ranging from six to eight inches in length, was found. They are superb examples of cane knives, the shape of a willow leaf, magnificently chipped and ground, with the cutting edge along one side instead of at the point.

With the cane knives was an exceptionally well-made whetstone used for sharpening the tools. In this case it might have been used to keep the edges sharpened on these particular cane knives, as all were deposited together. Cane knives excavated seem to be confined to this district.

Cane grows today in the bottom land, as it did during the time of the Mound Builders. It was used by them for many purposes, being split and woven, like the bottom of a wicker chair, in the construction of their houses, and in weaving mats and fabrics. Sharp-

[157]

ened shafts of the cane were made into fishing poles and to fit spears and arrows.

Wherever the soil here is exposed or disturbed, quantities of material are found. The ground is filled with artifacts. This, no doubt, is because the site is virgin, never having been disturbed by the plow or man, and because the aboriginal group, who occupied the only high ground where the Mississippi and Ohio Rivers meet, lived here for several hundred years, generation after generation. It is a pure type site.

Most bone implements found have been pale-white in color. The majority of those excavated here are the color of old ivory and have a lustrous polish and heavy patina, indicating long usage. Every day I am asked if we polish the bone implements. People can scarcely believe they have been in the ground for centuries and yet retain such a beautiful luster.

Bone implements have always intrigued me. They show such ingenuity on the part of the ancients. Who of us today would have the ingenuity to use a bird beak, even if it were an almost extinct ivory-billed woodpecker, for a weaving tool, or a fish spine or rib for a needle? The more I work with the early inhabitants of our country, the more respect I have for them. They were a wonderful race.

One day, while excavating, I left my trowel for a moment. An old gentleman was curious to see what I had been digging, so he started to dig and, unfortunately, broke one of the handsomest bone tools that has been excavated. In his haste and excitement when he saw the tool projecting through the dirt, he dug frantically, and pop! went the artifact. It was the last of a cache of awls, needles, skivers, and a spatula. The artifact that was broken is highly polished, tapering to a point, ten inches in length, and the artisan cleverly used the end of the deer bone out of which it was made for the handle, comparable to our paper knives.

We find from these discoveries that the male sex has always been a "dressy creature." This is true with the birds, the male having the more highly-colored plumage. It is equally true with the Mound Builder. The women, in those days, were the down-trodden race, just as we are today! The men wore the hairpins—sometimes they are carved out of shell; others are made out of a hard animal bone. Two beautifully polished ones excavated here are eleven inches in length, with both ends tapered.

One tool resembles a modern crochet hook. People are astonished at the similarity. It is four inches in length and the hook is almost worn away from usage; it must have woven lots of fabric and fish nets.

Deer astragalus, or the small bones from the foot of the deer, were polished and smoothed on rough sandstone or some other abrasive material and made into a cube resembling dice and used in games. An ancient game of the historic Indian was called "chungke." It was played by two men on a long, smooth piece of ground, around which the tribe sat as spectators. They used sticks bent at one end and a hard circular stone. Some which we have excavated are beautifully polished on all sides; others have convex and concave centers. They are called discoidals, and must have been kept carefully and handed down from generation to generation, as they are in such excellent condition. Archæologists are not positive whether the highly polished, perfect discoidals made by the prehistoric groups were used in ceremonials or games. Historic Indians loved games. It is interesting to see them play a guessing game with sticks and dice, where the spectators guess where the dice is hidden under the cloth. I have often watched them at various reservations.

Discoidals are made out of a great variety of materials—slate, marble, quartz, quartzite, granite, and greenstone. Some of the discoidals resemble the ancient lamp stones of the Eskimo.

Many caves in Europe have yielded beautiful bone implements. Tools and weapons of bone and ivory may be assumed to have preceded all but the rudest stone implements.

South of the Alps, in the caverns of Baoussé Roussé, personal ornaments of flint, ivory and shell were found, and in the Mentone Cave, a nearly perfect human skeleton, whose skull was decorated with an ornamental headdress of perforated shells (cyclonassa veritea) and canine teeth of the cervus elephus, originally strung, as is supposed, on a net for the hair. Across the forehead lay a large bone hairpin, made of the radius of a stag,

Mound Builder burials with pottery and other possessions

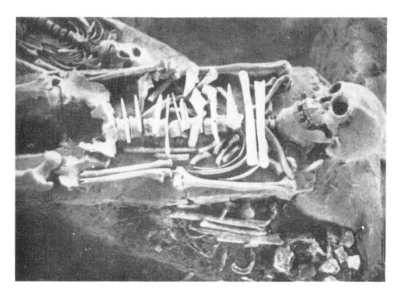

Leather Worker with bone implements, excavated at Wickliffe,
Kentucky

with the natural condyle retained as its head.

Excavations of the ancient Lake Dwellers of Switzerland have revealed combs, netting tools, pins, bodkins and other implements, made from bone. Germany, Scotland, England, Denmark, France, and other countries have revealed the same.

Bone tools were sharpened and rounded by rubbing in grooves, formed on a flat piece of sandstone. Recently we excavated a handsome one, very similar to one illustrated on Plate XXX in *Reliquiae aquitanicae, The Archæology of Périgord,* by Édouard Lartet and Henry Christy, London (1865–1875).

Antler tips of deer are very hard and were used to flake the flint in secondary chippings, the primary chipping having been done by percussion or blows of the stone maul or hammer. In all the mounds at the King site we find hollowed, polished antler tips, two to three inches in length. Many archæologists advance the opinion that they were used as arrow points to be attached to a spear or throwing stick. There was a groove around the top where they could be detached and used again and again.

When I first came to Kentucky, I was surprised to see men, women, and children in the fields in the spring of the year, with pointed wooden sticks, about eight inches in length, in their hands, with which they were punching holes at frequent intervals in the ground. Upon inquiry, I learned that they were taking the young plants from the tobacco beds and placing them in the holes, carefully packing the dirt around the base of the plant. They were doing exactly what had been done centuries before by the Red Men before any European knew of tobacco. This is evidenced by the many planting tools, made of bone, that we excavate, instead of the wooden type used today.

The early groups may have used wood also, but we have never found them. Those we have excavated are made of deer antlers, elk ribs, and various other animal bones, most of them being highly polished and rounded by long usage, the action of pushing the tool into the ground having polished the distal ends.

The first phalangeal bone of the hind foot of the deer was used for ornaments and whistles. Turkey bone callers, flutes, rings, and beautifully engraved ornaments were made from bone. A certain part of the anatomy of the raccoon was used as needles and perforators. Next to flint, bone was used for a majority of their utilitarian tools.

It was utilized in many ways. We have, without question, the greatest cross-section of the bone industry of any site excavated from the central basin. We have pieces illustrating sawing, whittling, carving, and rejected parts as evidence of their work.

One of the principal foods used by the Mound Builders was fish, and each excavation reveals many fishhooks made of bone. Some of them have a knob at the top, and others have grooves around them. Apparently the knob and grooves were made to facilitate attachment to the fish line. They are all sizes, some one inch in length with a very sharp barb, and others pointed like a harpoon. Some are carved.

Bone needles with eyes have been found in excavations in many countries. Speaking of the employment of sewing needles by the aborigines of the Reindeer period, in Dordogne, at Les Éyzies, Laugerie Basse, and at La Madelaine, large quantities of needles were found in company with harpoon heads of the barbed type.

In the Turner group of earthworks, on an altar in a trench of the embankment of the great enclosure, carved incised bones were excavated. The lines of the carving were originally filled with red pigment. "All of the carved bones were broken and badly injured by burning, but the upper part of one of the most interesting, which was probably made from a human ulna, has been pieced together. . . . It represents the head of an animal with upright ears, between which is an oval figure." [38]

When we eat we have a plate, a spoon, a knife, and a fork. The Central Basin folk, especially at this site, also had a plate, spoon, knife and fork. They used a polished deer ulna for a fork, a flint blade flaked for a knife, and mussel shells, which were much worn on the edges from usage, as a spoon; also a shallow plate made of terra cotta, often decorated inside and out with a leaf design which followed the same custom employed by our chinaware makers of today, who use roses to decorate soup plates.

Pieces of bone, quartz, flint, and shells were used as scalping knives. The omnipotent historic Indian, Powhatan, would punish any notorious enemy or trespasser and "causeth him to be tyed to a tree and with muscle shells or reedes the executioner cutteth off his joints, one after another ever casting what is cutt into the fier, then doth he proceede with shells and reedes to case the skyn from his head and face." [39]

The Central Basin groups would never have attained their degree of development, or had the great quantities of food they consumed, without the knowledge of working bone into artifacts for ceremonial purposes and for everyday use. This knowledge, without doubt, made their lives easier, and added to their comfort.

CHAPTER XVI

CONCLUSION

THE Mound Builder has gone—so unstable is the nature of all things mortal. But his Temple Mound remains, high overlooking the great Mississippi and Ohio Rivers. "I come here to find myself," as John Burroughs said. "It is so easy to get lost in the world."

It is springtime. In the distance the woods are filled with the colorful dogwood, red bud, wild plum, fragrant crab apple, and a profusion of wild flowers. The wild geese are flying in V formation down the rivers, as others must have flown hundreds of years ago, and at eventide the lone crane, with the swift beat of his wings, flies overhead.

I once saw the Colosseum in Rome by moonlight, and thought it one of the most impressive sights imaginable. But to go to the Burial Mound is equally impressive, no matter what the hour. It is elusive of analysis. I look at them in their dignity, surrounded by simple amulets, tools, and weapons, and am reminded of these lines from a beautiful poem—

"I have spread my dreams *under your feet;*
Tread softly, because you tread on my dreams."

NOTES

1. Sir Arthur Keith, *New Discoveries Relating to the Antiquity of Man,* p. 29.

2. Alês Hrdlička, *The Coming of Man from Asia in the Light of Recent Discoveries,* p. 463.

3. Dr. N. C. Nelson, "Antiquity of Man in America," in *The American Aborigines, Their Origin and Antiquity,* p. 130.

4. Frank Boas, "Relationships Between North-West America and North-East Asia," in *The American Aborigines, Their Origin and Antiquity,* p. 357.

5. Alês Hrdlička, "Coming of Man from Asia," in the *Annual Report Smithsonian Institution,* 1935, p. 469.

6. Diamond Jenness, *The Problem of the Eskimo,* p. 381.

7. Exodus XII, 37.

8. Alês Hrdlička, *op. cit.,* p. 468.

9. Dr. N. C. Nelson, *op. cit.,* p. 97.

10. Sir Arthur Keith, *Antiquity of Man,* Volume 2, pp. 459–749.

11. Dr. N. C. Nelson, *op. cit.,* p. 89.

12. F. J. Lafitau, *Mœurs des Sauvages Americains, Comparés aux Mœurs des Premiers Temps,* Tome I, Paris, 1724.

13. W. D. Funkhouser, *A Study of the Physical Anthropology and Pathology of the Osteological Material from the Norris Basin,* p. 250.

14. E. G. Squier and E. H. Davis, *Ancient Monuments of the Mississippi Valley,* pp. 126–127.

15. Henry R. Schoolcraft, *Historical and Statistical Information Respecting the History, Condition, and Prospects of the Indian Tribes of the United States: Collected and Prepared under the Direction of the Bureau of Indian Affairs,* Vol. I, p. 52.

16. Charles E. Brown, "The Preservation of the Man Mound." *The Wisconsin Archæologist,* Vol. VII, p. 140.

17. Dr. N. C. Nelson, *op. cit.,* p. 106.

NOTES

18. Clark Wissler, *Ethnological Diversity in America and Its Significance,* p. 183.

19. Captain John Smith, *True Travels,* Richmond Edition, 1819, p. 143.

20. William S. Webb, *An Archæological Survey of the Norris Basin,* p. 367.

21. Charles C. Willoughby, "The Turner Group of Earthworks, Hamilton Co., Ohio," in *Papers of the Peabody Museum,* Vol. VIII, p. 96.

22. Lucien Carr, *Dress and Ornaments of Certain American Indians,* p. 28.

23. Charles Jones, *Antiquities of the Southern Indians,* p. 74.

24. Erland Nordenskiold, *Origin of the Indian Civilizations in South America,* p. 252.

25. George Grant MacCurdy, *The Coming of Man,* p. 129.

26. M. C. and F. C. Cole, *The Story of Man,* p. 155.

27. James B. Griffin, *The Ceramic Remains from Norris Basin, Tennessee,* p. 253.

28. Charles E. Brown, "Wisconsin Spirit Stones," in *The Wisconsin Archæologist,* December 1908, Vol. VII, No. 4.

29. Edna St. Vincent Millay, "Travel," from *Second April.* Harper & Brothers, N.Y., p. 33.

30. Édouard Lartet and Henry Christy, *Reliquiae Aquitanicae—Contributions to Archæology and Palæontology.*

31. Liang Chi Chao, *Archæology in China,* p. 465.

32. Edouard Lartet and Henry Christy, *op. cit.*

33. Amelia Martinez Del Rio, *The Sun, the Moon and a Rabbit,* Sheed & Ward, 1935, p. 33.

34. J. W. Powell, *Myths of the Cherokee,* p. 240.

35. Claude Alloüez, *Relations des Jesuites,* Vol. 3, 1666 et 1667.

36. Robert Louis Stevenson, *Complete Poems,* Charles Scribner & Sons, p. 160.

37. E. G. Squier and E. H. Davis, *op. cit.,* p. 245.

38. Charles C. Willoughby, *op. cit.,* p. 8.

39. Émile P. Rivière, *Découvèrte d'un Squalletté Humain de L'Epoque Paléolithique dans les Caverns des Baoussé.*

SUGGESTED READINGS

Annual Reports of the Smithsonian Institution.

Archaeologia Americana, Vol. 1, 1820.

Black, Davidson, F.R.S., Royal Society of London, *The Croonian Lecture.*

Brown, F. Martin: *America's Yesterdays.*

Bushnell, David I., Jr.: Drawings by A. DeBatz in Louisiana, City of Washington. Published by the Smithsonian Institution.

Carr, L.: "Observations on the Crania from the Stone Graves of Tennessee," *Peabody Museum Report.* Vol. 2.

Catlin, George: *Illustrations of the Manners, Customs and Conditions of the North American Indians.* 2 vols. New York and London, 1848.

Champlain, Samuel de: *Voyages ou Journals et Découvertes de la Nouvelle France,* Tomes I–II, Paris, 1830.

Cole, Fay Cooper and Deuel, Thorne, *Rediscovering Illinois.* Univ. of Chicago Press, Chicago, Illinois.

Cushing, Frank: "Zuñi," *Second Annual Report of the Bureau of Ethnology,* 1880–81 J. W. Powell Director, Washington, D.C. Government Printing Office, 1883.

Marquette, Father Jacques, S.J.: *Discovery and Exploration of the Mississippi River.*

Hakluyt: Vol. 2, *Voyages of English Nation.*

Hrdlička, Alês: *Old Americans.*

Jenks, Albert Ernest: *Pleistocene Man in Minnesota.*

Keith, Sir Arthur: *The Antiquity of Man,* and *New Discoveries Relating to the Antiquity of Man,* Vols. I and II.

Kroeber, A. L.: *Anthropology.*

SUGGESTED READINGS

Mooney, *Myths of Cherokee* (U.S. Bureau of Ethnological Report).

Nadaillac, Marquis de: *L'Amérique Préhistorique.*

Shetrone, H. C.: *The Mound Builders.*

Smith, Harlan I.: *The Prehistoric Ethnology of a Kentucky Site.*

Thruston, Gates P.: *Antiquities of Tennessee.*

Waquet, Henri: (Archiviste du Finistère), *La Préhistoire et l'Époque Gallo-Romaine.*

Weidenreich, Franz: *Palæontologia Sinica.*

Wissler, Clark: *The American Indian.*

Young, Colonel Bennett H.: *The Prehistoric Man of Kentucky.*